First World War
and Army of Occupation
War Diary
France, Belgium and Germany

63 (ROYAL NAVAL) DIVISION
188 Infantry Brigade
1 Royal Marine Battalion
14 May 1916 - 30 April 1919

WO95/3110/1

The Naval & Military Press Ltd
www.nmarchive.com
Published in association with The National Archives

Published by

The Naval & Military Press Ltd

Unit 10 Ridgewood Industrial Park,

Uckfield, East Sussex,

TN22 5QE England

Tel: +44 (0) 1825 749494

www.naval-military-press.com

www.nmarchive.com

This diary has been reprinted in facsimile from the original. Any imperfections are inevitably reproduced and the quality may fall short of modern type and cartographic standards.

Contents

Document type	Place/Title	Date From	Date To
Heading	WO95/3110-1		
Heading	63rd Division 188th Infy Bde 1st Bn Royal Marines May 1916-April 1919		
Heading	War Diary of 1st Battalion, Royal Marines. From 14th May, 1916 To 30th June, 1916.		
War Diary	Mudros	14/05/1916	14/05/1916
War Diary	Marseilles	19/05/1916	20/05/1916
War Diary	Pont Remy Longpre	21/05/1916	01/06/1916
War Diary	Hersin	02/06/1916	21/06/1916
War Diary	Bois. de La Haie.	21/06/1916	25/06/1916
War Diary	Frevillers	25/06/1916	02/07/1916
War Diary	War Diary of 1st Battalion, Royal Marines From 1st July 1916 To 31st July 1916 Volume 2		
War Diary	Frevillers	01/07/1916	13/07/1916
War Diary	Fosse 10	13/07/1916	14/07/1916
War Diary	Front Line Trenches	14/07/1916	14/07/1916
War Diary	Front Line Trenches Angres II	15/07/1916	19/07/1916
War Diary	In Trenches Support	20/07/1916	20/07/1916
War Diary	Angres II In Support As For 20	21/07/1916	25/07/1916
War Diary	Angres II Front Line	25/07/1916	29/07/1916
War Diary	In Support	29/07/1916	31/07/1916
Heading	War Diary of 1st Battalion Royal Marines From 1st August 1916 To 31st August 1916 Volume III		
War Diary	Bully Grenay	01/08/1916	02/08/1916
War Diary	Front Line Trenches Angres II	03/08/1916	06/08/1916
War Diary	Bully Grenay & Fosse 10	06/08/1916	09/08/1916
War Diary	Front Line Angres II	10/08/1916	14/08/1916
War Diary	Fosse 10 & Bully Grenay	14/08/1916	17/08/1916
War Diary	Front Line	18/08/1916	21/08/1916
War Diary	Bde Support	22/08/1916	25/08/1916
War Diary	Front Line	26/08/1916	29/08/1916
War Diary	Bde Support	30/08/1916	31/08/1916
Heading	War Diary of 1st Battalion Royal Marines From 1st September 1916 To 30th September 1916 Volume IV		
War Diary	Bully Grenay	01/09/1916	02/09/1916
War Diary	Front Line Angres II	03/09/1916	03/09/1916
War Diary	Sub. Section	03/09/1916	06/09/1916
War Diary	Fosse 10 & Bully Grenay	07/09/1916	10/09/1916
War Diary	Front Line Angres II	11/09/1916	14/09/1916
War Diary	Fosse 10 & Bully Grenay	15/09/1916	18/09/1916
War Diary	Hersin	19/09/1916	20/09/1916
War Diary	Dieval	20/09/1916	30/09/1916
Heading	War Diary of 1st Battalion, Royal Marines From 1st October 1916 To 31st October 1916 Volume V		
War Diary	Dieval	01/10/1916	04/10/1916
War Diary	Mailley Wood	05/10/1916	08/10/1916
War Diary	Varennes	09/10/1916	09/10/1916
War Diary	Forceville	10/10/1916	17/10/1916
War Diary	Hedauville	18/10/1916	20/10/1916
War Diary	Engelbelmer	21/10/1916	22/10/1916

War Diary	Front Line Hamel Left	23/10/1916	25/10/1916
War Diary	Engelbelmer	26/10/1916	27/10/1916
War Diary	Front Line Hamel L	28/10/1916	30/10/1916
War Diary	Engelbelmer	31/10/1916	31/10/1916
Heading	War Diary of 1st Batt. Royal Marines From 1st November To 30th November Volume VI		
War Diary	Varennes	01/11/1916	05/11/1916
War Diary	Puchvillers	06/11/1916	07/11/1916
War Diary	Line	08/11/1916	08/11/1916
War Diary	Engelbelmer	09/11/1916	09/11/1916
War Diary	Varennes	10/11/1916	10/11/1916
War Diary	Line	11/11/1916	15/11/1916
War Diary	Puchvillers	16/11/1916	17/11/1916
War Diary	Gelaincourt	18/11/1916	18/11/1916
War Diary	Bernaville	19/11/1916	21/11/1916
War Diary	Cramont	22/11/1916	22/11/1916
War Diary	Froyelles	23/11/1916	23/11/1916
War Diary	Le Titre	24/11/1916	24/11/1916
War Diary	Morlay	25/11/1916	30/11/1916
Heading	War Diary of 1st Royal Marine Batt. From 1st Dec. 1916 To 31st Dec. 1916 Vol VII		
War Diary	Morlay	01/12/1916	13/12/1916
War Diary	Vron	14/12/1916	31/12/1916
Heading	War Diary of 1st Royal Marine Battalion From 1st January 1917 To 31st January 1917. Volume 8		
War Diary	Vron	01/01/1917	13/01/1917
War Diary	Saillybray	14/01/1917	14/01/1917
War Diary	Domvast	15/01/1917	15/01/1917
War Diary	Bois Bergues	16/01/1917	17/01/1917
War Diary	Beauquesne	18/01/1917	20/01/1917
War Diary	Englebelmer	21/01/1917	31/01/1917
Heading	War Diary of 1st Battalion Royal Marines From 1st February 1917 To 28th February 1917 Vol. IX		
War Diary	Englebelmer	01/02/1917	28/02/1917
Heading	War Diary of 1st Batt. Royal Marines Light Infantry From 1st March 1917 To 31st March 1917 Volume X		
War Diary	Brucehuts Aveloy	01/03/1917	19/03/1917
War Diary	Herrisart	20/03/1917	20/03/1917
War Diary	Gezaincourt	21/03/1917	21/03/1917
War Diary	Bouret	22/03/1917	22/03/1917
War Diary	Croisette	24/03/1917	24/03/1917
War Diary	Sains-Les-Pernes	25/03/1917	25/03/1917
War Diary	Ecquedecques	26/03/1917	26/03/1917
War Diary	Calonne-Sur-Lys	27/03/1917	27/03/1917
War Diary	Hesdigneul	28/03/1917	29/03/1917
War Diary	Labourse	30/03/1917	31/03/1917
Heading	War Diary of 1st Bn. Royal Marine Light Infantry From 1st April 1917 To 30 April 1917 Volume XI		
War Diary	La Bourse	01/04/1917	07/04/1917
War Diary	Angres II	08/04/1917	13/04/1917
War Diary	Angres II Sector	13/04/1917	20/04/1917
War Diary	Maroeuil	21/04/1917	22/04/1917
War Diary	Line	23/04/1917	30/04/1917
Heading	War Diary of 1st Battalion Royal Marines Light Infantry From 1st May, 1917, To 31st May, 1917 Volume XII		
War Diary	Ecoivres Revillers	01/05/1917	08/05/1917

War Diary	Conres	09/05/1917	09/05/1917
War Diary	Ecoivres	10/05/1917	18/05/1917
War Diary	Line	19/05/1917	31/05/1917
Heading	War Diary 1st Battalion Royal Marines Light Infantry From 1st June 1917 To 30th June 1917 Volume XIII		
War Diary	Reserve	01/06/1917	01/06/1917
War Diary	Trenches	02/06/1917	02/06/1917
War Diary	Gavrelle	03/06/1917	08/06/1917
War Diary	Roclincourt	09/06/1917	10/06/1917
War Diary	Maroieul	11/06/1917	30/06/1917
Heading	War Diary of 1st Battalion, Royal Marines Light Infantry From 1st July, 1917, To 31st July, 1917 Volume 14		
War Diary	Bray	01/07/1917	02/07/1917
War Diary	Roclincourt	03/07/1917	03/07/1917
War Diary	In The Line	04/07/1917	23/07/1917
War Diary	Maison Blanche	24/07/1917	30/07/1917
War Diary	Roclincourt	31/07/1917	31/07/1917
Heading	War Diary of 1st Battalion, Royal Marines Light Infantry, From 1st August, 1917, To 31st August, 1917 Volume XI		
War Diary	Beanchy Camp	01/08/1917	12/08/1917
War Diary	Naval Marine Trenches	13/08/1917	15/08/1917
War Diary	Front Line	15/08/1917	18/08/1917
War Diary	(Risval) Railway Cutting	19/08/1917	31/08/1917
Heading	War Diary of 1st Battalion, Royal Marines Light Infantry. From 1st September, 1917, To 30th September, 1917 Volume XII		
War Diary	Beverley Camp	01/09/1917	01/09/1917
War Diary	Roclincourt	02/09/1917	02/09/1917
War Diary	Line	03/09/1917	08/09/1917
War Diary	Maison Blanche	09/09/1917	12/09/1917
War Diary	Line	13/09/1917	16/09/1917
War Diary	Support Line	17/09/1917	17/09/1917
War Diary	Beverley Camp	18/09/1917	22/09/1917
War Diary	Bailleul Aux Cornailles	23/09/1917	23/09/1917
War Diary	Cornailles	24/09/1917	30/09/1917
Heading	War Diary of 1st Battalion, Royal Marines Light Infantry, From 1st October, 1917, To 31st October, 1917 Volume XVII		
War Diary	Bailleulau	01/10/1917	01/10/1917
War Diary	Cornailles	02/10/1917	10/10/1917
War Diary	Youveau Mond Wormhoudt	11/10/1917	24/10/1917
War Diary	Canal Bank Ypres	24/10/1917	24/10/1917
War Diary	In The Line	25/10/1917	27/10/1917
War Diary	Irish Farm	27/10/1917	31/10/1917
War Diary	War Diary From 1st November 1917, To, 30th November 1917. Vol 18		
War Diary	Dambre Camp	01/11/1917	05/11/1917
War Diary	Canal Bank (Yser)	06/11/1917	08/11/1917
War Diary	School Camp	09/11/1917	12/11/1917
War Diary	Winnezeele	12/11/1917	13/11/1917
War Diary	Ledringhem	14/11/1917	22/11/1917
War Diary	Brielen	23/11/1917	30/11/1917
Heading	War Diary Volume No XV 1/Battalion, Royal Marines Light Infantry. From 1/12/17 To 31/12/17		

War Diary	Garden City Camp Near Brielen	01/12/1917	05/12/1917
War Diary	Schools Camp Near Poperinghe	06/12/1917	08/12/1917
War Diary	Peselhock	09/12/1917	09/12/1917
War Diary	Beaulin Court	10/12/1917	13/12/1917
War Diary	Rocquigny	14/12/1917	14/12/1917
War Diary	Etricourt	15/12/1917	15/12/1917
War Diary	Lechelles	16/12/1917	21/12/1917
War Diary	Metg	22/12/1917	28/12/1917
War Diary	In The Line	29/12/1917	31/12/1917
Heading	War Diary of 1st Battalion, Royal Marines Light Infantry, From 1st January 1918 To 31st January 1918 Volume XX		
War Diary	Villers Plouich	01/01/1918	04/01/1918
War Diary	In The Line	05/01/1918	08/01/1918
War Diary	Metz	09/01/1918	12/01/1918
War Diary	In The Line	13/01/1918	16/01/1918
War Diary	Villers Plouich	17/01/1918	17/01/1918
War Diary	In The Line	18/01/1918	22/01/1918
War Diary	Villers Plouich	23/01/1918	23/01/1918
War Diary	Metz	24/01/1918	24/01/1918
War Diary	Roquigny	25/01/1918	31/01/1918
Heading	War Diary of 1st Battalion. Royal Marines Light Infantry From 1st February 1918 To 28th February 1918 Volume XVII		
War Diary	Rocquigny	01/02/1918	14/02/1918
War Diary	Eastwood Camp in Havrincourt Wood	15/02/1918	15/02/1918
War Diary	Havrincourt Wood	15/02/1918	16/02/1918
War Diary	Eastwood Camp Havrincourt Wood	17/02/1918	18/02/1918
War Diary	Couillet Sector Map Ref. La Vacuerie 1/10,000	19/02/1918	21/02/1918
War Diary	Pioneer Camp Lechelle	22/02/1918	23/02/1918
War Diary	Eastwood Camp Havrincourt Wood	24/02/1918	27/02/1918
War Diary	Support French Fllesquieres	28/02/1918	28/02/1918
Heading	188th Brigade 63rd Division 1st Battalion Royal Marine Light Infantry March 1918		
Heading	War Diary of 1st Battalion, Royal Marines. Volume XXI. From 1st March, 1918, To 31st March, 1918		
War Diary	Ribecourt Left In Support	01/03/1918	03/03/1918
War Diary	Ribecourt Left Frontline	04/03/1918	07/03/1918
War Diary	Eastwood Camp	08/03/1918	11/03/1918
War Diary	Support in Grand Ravine	12/03/1918	19/03/1918
War Diary	Frontline BN H Q. Screwtrench	20/03/1918	21/03/1918
War Diary	Flesquieres	21/03/1918	21/03/1918
War Diary	Havrincourt Wood	22/03/1918	23/03/1918
War Diary	Betincourt	24/03/1918	24/03/1918
War Diary	Martinpuich	25/03/1918	25/03/1918
War Diary	Thiepval	26/03/1918	26/03/1918
War Diary	Martinsart	27/03/1918	27/03/1918
War Diary	Aveluy Wood	28/03/1918	28/03/1918
War Diary	Forceville	29/03/1918	31/03/1918
Heading	War Diary 1st Battn. The Royal Marine Light Infantry April 1918		
Heading	War Diary of 1st Bn. Royal Marine Light Infantry Volume 22 From April 1st 1918 To April 30th 1918		
War Diary	Forceville	01/04/1918	02/04/1918
War Diary	Englebelmer	03/04/1918	05/04/1918
War Diary	Aveluywood	05/04/1918	07/04/1918

War Diary	Forceville	08/04/1918	09/04/1918
War Diary	Aveluy Wood	10/04/1918	11/04/1918
War Diary	Forceville	12/04/1918	13/04/1918
War Diary	Arqueves	14/04/1918	30/04/1918
Heading	War Diary of 1st Battalion, Royal Marines. Volume XXIII From 1st May 1918 To 31st May 1918		
War Diary	Arqueves	01/05/1918	08/05/1918
War Diary	Support In Front of Hamel	08/05/1918	14/05/1918
War Diary	Front Line Before Hamel	14/05/1918	18/05/1918
War Diary	Front Line Hamel Sector Left	18/05/1918	19/05/1918
War Diary	Front Line Before Hamel	19/05/1918	20/05/1918
War Diary	Forceville	20/05/1918	24/05/1918
War Diary	Line	24/05/1918	31/05/1918
Heading	War Diary Of 1st Battn. Royal Marines. Vol. XXIV 1st June 1918 To 30th June 1918		
War Diary	Support	01/06/1918	06/06/1918
War Diary	V.2.d. Map Ref57	06/06/1918	15/06/1918
War Diary	Herissart	16/06/1918	22/06/1918
War Diary	Serve Aumont El Sector	23/06/1918	30/06/1918
Heading	War Diary Of 1st Battn. Royal Marines Vol. XXV 1st July 1918 To 31st July 1918		
War Diary	Divisional Reserve	01/07/1918	01/07/1918
War Diary	Beaumont Hamel Sector	02/07/1918	08/07/1918
War Diary	Auchon-Villers	06/07/1918	13/07/1918
War Diary	Support Beaumont-Hamel Sector	14/07/1918	25/07/1918
War Diary	Arqueves	26/07/1918	29/07/1918
War Diary	Authie	30/07/1918	31/07/1918
Heading	1st Battalion Royal Marines War Diary 1st August 1918 To 31st August 1918 Vol 27		
War Diary	Authie	01/08/1918	04/08/1918
War Diary	Auchells	05/08/1918	05/08/1918
War Diary	Brown Line Acheux	06/08/1918	10/08/1918
War Diary	Contay	11/08/1918	14/08/1918
War Diary	Henu	15/08/1918	19/08/1918
War Diary	Souastre	20/08/1918	20/08/1918
War Diary	British Front Line Before Ablaizonville	20/08/1918	20/08/1918
War Diary	Logeast Wood	22/08/1918	23/08/1918
War Diary	Blueline	24/08/1918	24/08/1918
War Diary	Loupart Wood	25/08/1918	28/08/1918
War Diary	Mirumont	29/08/1918	30/08/1918
War Diary	Boiry St Rictrude	31/08/1918	31/08/1918
Heading	1st Battalion Royal Marines. War Diary. Volume XXV 1.9.18 To 30.9.18		
War Diary	Boiry St Rictrude	01/09/1918	01/09/1918
War Diary	Mitchon From U10a To Queant	02/09/1918	03/09/1918
War Diary	Buissy Switch	04/09/1918	07/09/1918
War Diary	U19d8.5	08/09/1918	08/09/1918
War Diary	Gouy-En-Artois	09/09/1918	18/09/1918
War Diary	Nr Croisilles	19/09/1918	25/09/1918
War Diary	Croisilles	26/09/1918	26/09/1918
War Diary	Inaction Over In Canal Du Nord	27/09/1918	27/09/1918
War Diary	Anneux	28/09/1918	28/09/1918
War Diary	Between Fontaine Cantaing	29/09/1918	29/09/1918
War Diary	Highground Over Looking Proville And Fly As Paris	30/09/1918	01/10/1918
Heading	1st Battalion Royal Marines War Diary October 1st To 31st 1918 Vol. VI		

War Diary	Highground Overlooking Proville And Fbg De Paris	01/10/1918	01/10/1918
War Diary	Nr Anneux	02/10/1918	08/10/1918
War Diary	G.16.a.&.c	08/10/1918	08/10/1918
War Diary	Nr.Niergnies	08/10/1918	09/10/1918
War Diary	Morchies	10/10/1918	11/10/1918
War Diary	Pierremont	12/10/1918	22/10/1918
War Diary	Ambrines	23/10/1918	31/10/1918
War Diary	1st Battalion Royal Marines War Diary Vol. VII November 1st-30th 1918		
War Diary	Ambrines	01/11/1918	01/11/1918
War Diary	Evin-Malmaison	02/11/1918	09/11/1918
War Diary	Aetine Operation	10/11/1918	11/11/1918
War Diary	Lers St Hslain	12/11/1918	18/11/1918
War Diary	Move	19/11/1918	20/11/1918
War Diary	Lers St Hislain	21/11/1918	26/11/1918
War Diary	Eugies	27/11/1918	30/11/1918
Heading	1st Battalion Royal Marines. War Diary Vol. 8 December 1st To 31st 1918.		
War Diary	Eugies	01/12/1918	11/12/1918
War Diary	La Bouverie	12/12/1918	31/12/1918
Heading	1st Bn. Marines. War Diary Vol. 9 January 31st 1919		
War Diary	La Bouverie And Eugies Belgium	01/01/1919	31/01/1919
Miscellaneous	Adjutant General 3rd Echelon	03/03/1919	03/03/1919
Heading	1st. Bn. Royal Marines War Diary Vol. 10 February 1919		
War Diary	Eugies & La Bouverie Belgium	01/02/1919	28/02/1919
Heading	1st Bn Royal Marines War Diary Vol. 11 March 1919		
War Diary	La Bouverie Belgium	01/03/1919	31/03/1919
Heading	1st. Battn. Royal Marines. War Diary Vol 12 April 1919		
War Diary	La Bouverie Belgium	01/04/1919	30/04/1919

WO95/3110 (1)

WO95/3110 (1)

63RD DIVISION
188TH INFY BDE

1ST BN ROYAL MARINES

MAY 1916-APR 1919

ABSORBED 2BN 1918 APR

3rd Brigade Royal Naval Division
Later 190 Brigade

1st R Marines
June
Vol 1

"Confidential"

Headquarters, 1st Royal Marines,
1st Brigade, Royal Naval Division,
12th July, 1916.

War Diary

of

1st Battalion, Royal Marines.

from

14th May, 1916.

to

30th June, 1916.

apr 19

To The A.Gs Office,

3rd Echelon.

F J W Cartwright

Major, R.M.L.I.,
Comdg 1st Royal Marines.

Army Form C. 2118.

Instructions regarding War Diaries and Intelligence Summaries are contained in F. S. Regs., Part II. and the Staff Manual respectively. Title pages will be prepared in manuscript.

WAR DIARY
~~or~~
~~INTELLIGENCE SUMMARY.~~
(Erase heading not required.)

Place	Date	Hour	Summary of Events and Information	Remarks and references to Appendices
MUDROS	14/5/16		The Battn. Embarked on board H.M.T. "ARAGON" during the forenoon. Strength 25 Officers (including Surgeon & Chaplain) and 1021 Other Ranks. Ten O.R. of 1st Line Transport left with Div: Train for care of officers chargers.	
			The transport sailed midnight 14/15 May. During voyage very fine weather. No attack by submarines, nor were any submarines sighted.	
MARSEILLES	19/5/16		Arrived Marseilles 6.30 a.m. Battn. left "ARAGON" at 2 p.m. and entrained. Destination PONT RÉMY. Train left MARSEILLES at 4 p.m. (2/Lt. E. Cohen was discharged to Hospital on arrival of Transport).	
	20/5/16		En route. Nothing of special interest to mention	
PONT & RÉMY. LONGPRÉ	21/5/16		Arrived PONT RÉMY at 5.15 p.m. and proceeded to LONGPRÉ where Battn. was billeted arriving 8 p.m.	
"	22/5/16 to 31/5/16		Re-equipping and Company training. On the 26th inst. Lieut. Col. E. J. Strond reassumed command of the Battn. until the 31st inst. when Major J. S. W. Cartwright took over command, on the former to Act. Brigadier of 3rd Brigade vice Brig. Gen. C. N. Trotman to leave.	
"	31/5/16		Received orders to entrain on 1st June for BARLIN.	
"	1/6/16		Left LONGPRÉ 11 am for PONT RÉMY arriving there 1.15 p.m. Entrained and left for BARLIN at 3.47 p.m. Arrived BARLIN 9.30 p.m. thence by route march to HERSIN arriving 12.15 am 2nd inst.	

T.2134. Wt. W708–776. 500000. 4/15. Sir J. C. & S.

Instructions regarding War Diaries and Intelligence Summaries are contained in F. S. Regs., Part II. and the Staff Manual respectively. Title pages will be prepared in manuscript.

WAR DIARY

~~or~~

~~INTELLIGENCE SUMMARY.~~

(Erase heading not required.)

Army Form C. 2118.

Place	Date	Hour	Summary of Events and Information	Remarks and references to Appendices
HERSIN	2/6/16		Having put up in temporary billets for night of 1/2nd, companies were allotted to billets on 2nd.	
"	3/6/16		The Battn together with 1/ANSON Bn were inspected by G.O.C., 1st Army at MAISNIL	
"	4/6/16		Training. "A" & "C" Coys put through the Gas Chamber & under orders to proceed to trenches for training.	
"	5/6/16		"A" & "C" Coys: proceeded to trenches at 8am. "A" Coy attached to E Lancs Regt & "C" Coy to Sherwood Foresters of the	ANGRES I SECTION
"	"		24th Inf. Bde. of 23rd Divn. <u>Casualties</u>. "A" Coy: Ch 17(S) Pte A.S. Drew wounded by shell & died in Advd Dressing Stn.	
"	"		"B" & "D" Coys on night working parties.	
"	6/6/16		Bn H.Q., "B" & "D" Coys put through Gas Chamber. 3 officers, 1 W.O. & 52 O.R. rejoined Bn from Base to England.	
"	7/6/16		D Coy training. B Coy on working parties. <u>Casualties</u>. "C" Coy Ply 655(S) Pte. B. Bottomley & Ply 789(S) Pte B. Pulman wounded.	
"	8/6/16		B & D Coys: proceeded to trenches at 8am. B Coy attached to Sherwood Foresters and D Coy to E Lancs Regt.	
"			A & C Coys from trenches to HERSIN. O.C. Bn & Adjt to trenches, ~~[illegible]~~ remaining ~~for the night and Adjt~~ till the evening are	
"			~~returning~~. <u>Casualties</u>. D Coy Ply 16898 Pte A. Camp (suffering from shell shock)	
"	9/6/16		A & C Coys, baths and training	
"	10/6/16		A & C Coys training. O.C. Bn & Adjt proceeded to trenches at 4.30pm. O.C. remaining for the night. Adjt returning during the night	
"	11/6/16		Bn H.Q., "A" & "C" Coys: to trenches for further instruction, B & D Coys still remaining on, i.e. whole Battn	

Instructions regarding War Diaries and Intelligence Summaries are contained in F. S. Regs., Part II. and the Staff Manual respectively. Title pages will be prepared in manuscript.

WAR DIARY
or
INTELLIGENCE SUMMARY.
(Erase heading not required.)

Army Form C. 2118.

Place	Date	Hour	Summary of Events and Information	Remarks and references to Appendices
HERSIN	11/6/16		in trenches for instruction disposed as follows:- "A" & "D" Coys. attached to Worcester Regt. "B" & "C" Coys attached to Northamptonshire Regt. - "D" & "C" in front line, "A" & "B" in support line. BN. H.Q. attached to BN H.Q. North'n/Regt. Casualties D Coy. Ch 861(S) Pte A Blackburn, Ch 819(S) Pte A Hooker, Po 904(S) Pte J. Hyslop wounded.	
"	12/6/16		Adjt. to HERSIN from trenches (& Bn H.Q.) "A" & "B" Coys from trenches to BOIS de la HAIE	
"	13/6/16		"C" & "D" Coys from trenches to BOIS de la HAIE. (Relieved in trenches by 2 Coys: 2/RM). BN H.Q. from HERSIN to BOIS de la HAIE. The Battn. then on the 13th inst. relieved the HOWE BN who were previously encamped in the wood, and are under the orders of the O.C 4/R.W.F for work on the completion of the BAJOLLE & MAISTRE LINES of defence. The 1st Line Transport & Q.M. Department are billeted at HOUDAIN.	
	14/6/16 to 18/6/16		Coys: employed under orders of O.C. 4/R.W.F. on above mentioned works.	
	18/6/16		BOIS de la HAIE. Inspection of Clothing & Equipment. Divine Service.	
	19.6.16		" " " Working under the Orders of the O.C. 4/R.W.F. as for 13.6.16	
	20.6.16		" " " —— Ditto ——	
	——		7 Officers, & 388 O.R. under command of Capt V. D. Loxley, proceeded to FREVILLERS P.M. this day, for training	
	21.6.16		The remainder of Batt. left at BOIS de la HAIE working under orders of O.C. 4/R.W.F.; others training at FREVILLERS. move. Qr master's Dept. & first-line transport, from HOUDAIN to FREVILLERS P.M. this day.	Con

T2134. Wt. W708—776. 500000. 4/15. Sir J. C. & S.

Instructions regarding War Diaries and Intelligence Summaries are contained in F. S. Regs., Part II. and the Staff Manual respectively. Title pages will be prepared in manuscript.

WAR DIARY
or
INTELLIGENCE SUMMARY.
(Erase heading not required.)

Army Form C. 2118.

Place	Date	Hour	Summary of Events and Information	Remarks and references to Appendices
BOIS de la HAIE.	21.6.16	Continued	Move. 3rd Bde Hd Quarters from FREVILLERS to FRESNICOURT. P.M. this day 3rd Trench Mortar Battery from BAJUS to HERMIN. 3rd Bde Bomb School from LA COMTE to CUVIGNY this day	
— " —	22.6.16		7 Officers & 388 O.R. Training at FREVILLERS, remainder of Battn working under orders of O.C. 4/R.W.F.	
— " —	23.6.16		As for 22.6.16	
	24.6.16		As for 23.6.16. 1 Officer & 23 O.R. rejoined Battn this day, from Bombing Instruction	
— " —	25.6.16		Relieved by the 14th Worcester (Pioneers) in BOIS de la HAIE. & joined remainder of Battn at FREVILLERS, P.M. this day, & went into billets	
FREVILLERS				
— " —	26.6.16		The whole Battn commenced a strenuous course of training. Lieut G. H. le Grove & Lieut H. L. Froward	to England
— " —	27.6.16		Battn Training	
— " —	28.6.16		— " —	
— " —	29.6.16		— " —	
— " —	30.6.16		— " —	
— " —	1.7.16		— " — } carried forward	
— " —	2.7.16		— " — }	

T2134. Wt. W708—776. 500000. 4/15. Sir J. C. & S.

July

63

1st R Marines

Vol 5

"Confidential"

Head Qrs, 1st Royal Marines
188th Inf. Bde. 63rd (R.N.) Divn
1st August 1916

War Diary
of
1st Battalion, Royal Marines
from
1st July 1916
to
31st July 1916
Volume 2

Hd Qrs
63rd (R.N) Divn

C.J. Hvord.

Colonel R.M.L.I.
Comdg 1/Royal Marines

Instructions regarding War Diaries and Intelligence Summaries are contained in F. S. Regs., Part II. and the Staff Manual respectively. Title pages will be prepared in manuscript.

WAR DIARY
or
INTELLIGENCE SUMMARY.
(Erase heading not required.)

Army Form C. 2118.

Place	Date	Hour	Summary of Events and Information	Remarks and references to Appendices
FREVILLERS	1.4.16		Battn training by Companies [initials]	
— " —	2.4.16			
FREVILLERS	3.4.16		Battalion training by Companies. Courses of instruction under Battn Instructors in wiring, Bombing, Lewis Guns, Physical Training & bayonet fighting, Sniping & Scouting. The Corps Commander visited here, & inspected some of the billets. Capt A.K. Evans joined the 1st Brigade for training in "Staff Work". [initials]	
— " —	4.4.16		——— Training as above ——— [initials]	
— " —	5.4.16		——— " ——— [initials]	
— " —	6.4.16		——— " ——— [initials]	
— " —	7.4.16		The whole Battn (including 1st line transport) proceeded by Route march to BOIS d' OLHAIN (Ref. map France 36B Edition 6) Carried out an Outpost Scheme, returning to Billets at 4.30 P.M. 3rd Brigade R.N.D. now 1st Inf. Bde R.N.D. Commencing this day [initials]	
— " —	8.4.16		Battalion training as on 3.4.16 [initials]	
— " —	9.4.16		Divine Service & Inspection of equipment & kit. Disinfection of all Battn Blankets & Clothing [initials]	
— " —	10.4.16		Battalion training as on the 3.4.16 [initials]	
— " —	11.4.16		Training as for 10.4.16 [initials]	
— " —	12.4.16		Preparing to move. O.C. Companies & Lewis Gun Teams, with Guns & ammunition proceeded to HERSIN P.M. this day. [initials]	

T2134. Wt. W708—776. 500000. 4/15. Sir J. C. & S.

Army Form C. 2118.

WAR DIARY
or
INTELLIGENCE SUMMARY.
(Erase heading not required.)

Instructions regarding War Diaries and Intelligence Summaries are contained in F. S. Regs., Part II. and the Staff Manual respectively. Title pages will be prepared in manuscript.

Place	Date	Hour	Summary of Events and Information	Remarks and references to Appendices
FREVILLERS	13.4.16		Battalion vacated billets at FREVILLERS at 8.0 A.m. and marched via	
FOSSE 10	13.4.16		HERMIN, FRESNICOURT, and HERSIN to FOSSE 10. arriving there at 12.30 P.M. The marching was good, averaging 3½ miles per hour. The whole Battn was billeted by 1.30 P.m., less Transport and Q' master's dept, who were billeted at BARLIN. The following Officers joined the Battn P.M. yesterday. Lieut J. Neville Leon. 2nd Lieut J. E. Cornish, 2nd Lieut S/ H. Prynne, 2nd Lieut T. C. Callendar, 2nd Lieut C. E. H. Collis, 2nd Lieut Archibald Pike, 2nd Lieut C. W. Martin, 2nd Lieut H. E. R. Upham, 2nd Lieut Cecil Rugg, 2nd Lieut F. W. Goldie, 2nd Lieut E. G. C. Coulson	
FOSSE 10	14.4.16		Vacated billets at 1.0 P.M. and proceeded to FRONT LINE TRENCHES, ANGRES II Sub Section relieved the 24th LONDON Regt. Temp Major V. D. LOXLEY Wounded in leg (Slight)	
FRONT LINE TRENCHES	14.4.16		Lieut W. C. A. Elliott went out to patrol NO MANS LAND at about 10.15 P.M. + has not returned	
FRONT LINE TRENCHES ANGRES II	15.4.16		Quiet during day. Temp Major V. D. LOXLEY to Hospital. One of the Patrol who went out with Lieut W. C. A. ELLIOTT returned to our lines + reported that they were fired on by Enemy M. Guns, + that Lieut Elliott was wounded. Patrols went out from 10.0 pm (15.4.16) to 1.30 Am (16.4.16) searching for the missing patrol, but without success.	

T2134. Wt. W708–776. 500000. 4/15. Sir J. C. & S.

Instructions regarding War Diaries and Intelligence Summaries are contained in F. S. Regs., Part II. and the Staff Manual respectively. Title pages will be prepared in manuscript.

WAR DIARY
or
INTELLIGENCE SUMMARY.
(Erase heading not required.)

Army Form C. 2118.

Place	Date	Hour	Summary of Events and Information	Remarks and references to Appendices
			Map reference. Sheet 36 B. S.E.	
FRONT LINE TRENCHES. ANGRES II	16.4.16		Brigadier General R.E.S. PRENTICE assumed Command of the 1st Brigade R.N.D. this day, vice Colonel E.J. STROUD RMLI. The 141st Infantry Bde carried out a raid on apex of enemy Salient at M.32.d.0.3. 1st Naval Bde demonstrated opposite Salient M.26.C. Artillery laid barrage round point of attack, across Salient in M.26.C, & E. of BULLY CRATERS. Enemy Artillery reply feeble. Colonel E.J. STROUD assumed Command of 1/Rm. this day	[initials]
— " —	17.4.16		In Trenches. Quiet	[initials]
— " —	18.4.16		One of the missing Patrol returned to our lines, & reported that Lieut H.C.A. ELLIOTT died on the night of 15th–16th inst., from wounds received on the night of the 14–15th inst. No further trace of Lieut ELLIOTT can be found, & he has been reported "Missing, believed Killed". Quiet	[initials]
— " —	19.4.16		A Quiet 24 hours	[initials]
In Trenches / " Support	20.4.16		Relieved by 2/Rm Batt. relief completed smoothly by 4.0 pm. Batt moved into Support. 1 Coy in CAP DE PONT, 1 Coy in MECHANICS TRENCH, 2 Coys & Batt Hd Qrs at BULLY GRENAY. Name of Division changed from 'Royal Naval Division' to The 63rd (Royal Naval) Division. Name of Brigade from 1st Bde R.N.D. to 188 Bde	[initials]

T2134. Wt. W708—776. 500000. 4/15. Sir J. C. & S.

Instructions regarding War Diaries and Intelligence Summaries are contained in F. S. Regs., Part II. and the Staff Manual respectively. Title pages will be prepared in manuscript.

WAR DIARY
or
INTELLIGENCE SUMMARY.
(Erase heading not required.)

Army Form C. 2118.

Place	Date	Hour	Summary of Events and Information	Remarks and references to Appendices
ANGRES II				
In Support	21.4.16		Batth went through Bde Baths General Clean up	
as for 20th				
— " —	22.4.16		— do —	
— " —	23.4.16		Divine Service, Inspection of Equipment &c	
— " —	24.4.16		Ordinary Fatigue Work, Working Parties &c	
—	25.4.16		Ordinary Support duties up to 1.0 P.M. Batth left billets at 1.0 pm, & proceeded	
ANGRES II Front-LINE			to relieve 2/R.M. Batth in FIRING LINE ANGRES II. Sub-Section relief carried	
			out Sooothly by 4.0 pm.	
— " —	26.4.16		In front line trenches Wiring in front of whole Sector. No Casualties	
			A Quiet day.	
— " —	27.4.16		In front line trenches, ordinary trench routine. Very Quiet day	
— " —	28.4.16		In front line trenches. Ordinary trench routine A little enemy Artillery	
			Activity. One Casualty (Slightly wounded)	
— " —	29.4.16		In front line trenches up to 3.0 pm. relieved by 2/Rm Batth relief	
			Completed by 4.0 pm. One Casualty (Slightly wounded)	
In Support	— " —	P.M.	Moved into Billets at BULLY GRENAY (two Companies) One Coy at MECHANICS	

G.T.O

Instructions regarding War Diaries and Intelligence Summaries are contained in F. S. Regs., Part II. and the Staff Manual respectively. Title pages will be prepared in manuscript.

WAR DIARY
or
INTELLIGENCE SUMMARY.
(Erase heading not required.)

Army Form C. 2118.

Place	Date	Hour	Summary of Events and Information	Remarks and references to Appendices
ANGRES II		pm	MECHANICS	
In Support	29.7.16		and one coy at CAP DE PONT, + CORON DAIX HL	
—"—	30.7.16		General Support duties, Inspections, Divine Service, Baths + general clean up no casualties HL	
—"—	31.7.16		As for yesterday. Lieut J. Neville Lion, and 2nd Lieut J. E. Cornish proceeded to join Medium Trench Mortar School (1st Army). P.M. this day HL	

T2134. Wt. W708—776. 500000. 4/15. Sir J. C. & S.

Confidential

HdQrs 1st Royal Marines
188th Inf Bde. 63rd (RN) Dn
1st Sept 1916

War Diary
of
1st Battalion Royal Marines
from
1st August 1916
to
31st August 1916.

HdQrs
63rd (RN) Divn

F J W Cartwright.
Major RMLI
Comdg 1/Royal Marines

Volume III (August) 16.

Instructions regarding War Diaries and Intelligence Summaries are contained in F. S. Regs., Part II. and the Staff Manual respectively. Title pages will be prepared in manuscript.

WAR DIARY
or
INTELLIGENCE SUMMARY.
(Erase heading not required.)

Army Form C. 2118.

1st Royal Marine Battalion

Place	Date	Hour	Summary of Events and Information	Remarks and references to Appendices
BULLY GRENAY & FOSSE 10	1·8·16		Battalion in Reserve ANGRES II Sub-Section. "A" & "B" Coys in FOSSE 10, "C" & "D" Coys in BULLY GRENAY. 2nd Lieut H. S. R. Upham, & 10. O. R. to Bde Bomb School for a Course of instruction. Quarter Master's Stores, & 1st line transport at BARLIN. Head Quarters at FOSSE 10.	[initials]
FOSSE 10 & BULLY GRENAY	2·8·16	AM	Battn distributed as for 1·8·16 (In Reserve	
		PM	" moved into FRONT LINE TRENCHES, relieving 2/Rm Battn in ANGRES II Sub Section. Relief completed by 4·0 PM. Casualties One. O. R. (Wounded)	[initials]
FRONT LINE TRENCHES ANGRES II	3·8·16		Ordinary FRONT LINE routine. Notification of death of 962(S) Pte A. J. Wilson, wounded yesterday (2 8 16). An explosion occurred in a "Dug-out" in which was stored about 100 rounds of Stokes Gun ammunition. The "Dug out" was completely wrecked & 1 Corpl & 4 Ptes of the 188 T. M. Battery were killed. No knowledge as to how explosion occurred. Captain A. K. Evans R.M.L.I. Appointed G.S.O.3. 63rd (RN) Division, & is struck off strength of Battn. Lieut J. C. Watkins rejoined Battn from Bde "Bomb School". The provisional promotion of Temp 2nd Lieut R. B. Walker to Temp Capt. is Cancelled B. R. O. 2·8·16	[initials] [initials]

T2134. Wt. W708—776. 500000. 4/15. Sir J. C. & S.

Instructions regarding War Diaries and Intelligence Summaries are contained in F. S. Regs., Part II. and the Staff Manual respectively. Title pages will be prepared in manuscript.

WAR DIARY
or
INTELLIGENCE SUMMARY.
(Erase heading not required.)

Army Form C. 2118.

1/R.M. Battn. 188 Brigade

Place	Date	Hour	Summary of Events and Information	Remarks and references to Appendices
	Continued			
	3.8.16		2nd Lieut S. J. H. Bryane to Hospital.	[initials]
FRONT LINE ANGRES II	4.8.16		Ordinary FRONT LINE Routine. Temp Captain L. F. Morse Rejoined Battn from Divisional Gas School. Quiet. Casualties. One Pte Killed by rifle Grenade.	[initials]
—"—	5.8.16		No Change in the Situation. Constant patrolling during hours of darkness no enemy encountered. 2nd Lieut B. A. Sims, & 3 O.R. wounded, & evacuated to Hospital	[initials]
FRONT LINE ANGRES II & BULLY GRENAY & FOSSE 10	6.8.16		Battn relieved in ANGRES II by 2/R.M. Battn, relief completed by 12.0 noon moved into Reserve. Hd Qrs C & D. to FOSSE 10, A & B to BULLY GRENAY, taking over billets vacated by 2/Rm. 2nd Lieut C. R. H. Collie to Bde Bomb School together with 10. O.R. for Course of instruction. 2nd Lieut H. E. R. Upham & 10 O.R. rejoined Battn from Bomb School	[initials]
BULLY GRENAY & FOSSE 10	7.8.16		Battalion in Reserve. Baths, Working parties &c	[initials]
BULLY GRENAY & FOSSE 10	8.8.16		Battalion in Reserve. Working parties. 10 O.R. detached to 188 M. G. Coy. Hd Qrs this day	[initials]

T2134. Wt. W708—776. 500000. 4/15. Sir J. C. & S.

Instructions regarding War Diaries and Intelligence Summaries are contained in F. S. Regs., Part II. and the Staff Manual respectively. Title pages will be prepared in manuscript.

WAR DIARY
or
INTELLIGENCE SUMMARY.
(Erase heading not required.)

Army Form C. 2118.

1st Royal Marine Battn

Place	Date	Hour	Summary of Events and Information	Remarks and references to Appendices
BULLY GRENAY & FOSSE 10	9.8.16		In Reserve. Lieut & (T) Capt M. C. Browne D.S.C. rejoined Battn from 1st Army School, also 1. O.R. EEL	
FRONT LINE ANGRES II	10.8.16		Battn vacated billets at BULLY GRENAY, & FOSSE 10, & moved into FRONT LINE, relieving 2/R.M. Battn; Relief completed smoothly by 11.30 A.M. Enemy Artillery active about 3.15 P.M. to 3.35 P.M. Two O.R. accidentally wounded by the premature explosion of a Rifle Grenade. EEL	
FRONT LINE ANGRES II	11.8.16		A very quiet day. Six Officers of the H.A.C. were shown over the Sub-Section. Colonel E. J. Stroud R.M.L.I. met with an accident, & badly sprained his Ankle. Was sent down to Field Ambulance at 9.35 P.M. Major F. W. Cartwright R.M.L.I. therefore assumed Command of the Battn. A good deal of Aerial Activity on both sides, between 6.0 & 8.0 P.M. EEL	
FRONT LINE ANGRES II	12.8.16		Quiet 24 hours. Ordinary trench routine. 2nd Lieut C. R. N. Collis & 10 O.R. rejoined Battn from Course of Instruction at Bde Bomb School. Two O.R. proceeded to LE TOUQUET, for a Course of Instruction in Lewis Guns. EEL	
FRONT LINE ANGRES II	13.8.16		A fair amount of Artillery Activity on both sides. A Court of Enquiry was held to Investigate & Report the circumstances under which the following were accidentally	

T2134. Wt. W708—776. 500000. 4/15. Sir J. C. & S.

Army Form C. 2118.

Instructions regarding War Diaries and Intelligence Summaries are contained in F. S. Regs., Part II. and the Staff Manual respectively. Title pages will be prepared in manuscript.

WAR DIARY
or
INTELLIGENCE SUMMARY.
(*Erase heading not required.*)

1st Battalion Royal Marines

Place	Date	Hour	Summary of Events and Information	Remarks and references to Appendices
FRONT LINE ANGRES II	13.8.16		Accidentally Wounded Ch/1860 Pte D.A.A. Phillips, & Ply/(S) Pte T. Welsh. President Lieut & (T) Capt W.A. Pinkerton R.M.L.I. Members (T) 2nd Lieut Wm Golding R.M.* (T) 2nd Lieut G. West R.M. The finding of the Court was:- That the above named Privates were wounded by the Premature explosion of a Newton Pippin Rifle Grenade. (T) 2nd Lieut F.W. Goldie, & 10 O.R. to Bde Bomb School, for a Course of Instruction.	
FRONT Line ANGRES II FOSSE 10 & BULLY GRENAY	14.8.16		Battn relieved in FRONT LINE by 2/R.M. Relief Completed by 12.0 NOON. Moved into Bde Reserve, taking over Billets from 2/R.M. Hd Qrs 'A' & 'B' Coys & Lewis Guns at FOSSE 10, 'C' & 'D' Coys at BULLY GRENAY. Quartermaster's Stores, & First Line Transport at BARLIN.	
—"—	15.8.16		In Bde Reserve as above. 16 O.R. detached to 255 Tunnelling Coy. at Pt SAINS. 25 O.R. rejoined Battn from 255 Tunnelling Coy. No 12444 L/Corpl Pincombe 10th Hussars attached to Battn for duty, & report, with a view to his obtaining a Commission in H.M. Forces.	
—"—	16.8.16		In Reserve as above	
BULLY GRENAY	17.8.16		Battn moved into Bde Support, relieving Howe Battn. Hd Qrs ~~A & B~~ 'C' & 'D' Coys, & Lewis Guns at Bully, 'A' Coy in CORON D'AIX, & CAP DE PONT, 'B' Coy. MECHANICS. L. Guns relieved L. Guns 2/R.M. in FRONT LINE at 3.0 P.M.	

T2134. Wt. W708—776. 500000. 4/15. Sir J. C. & S.

Instructions regarding War Diaries and Intelligence Summaries are contained in F. S. Regs., Part II. and the Staff Manual respectively. Title pages will be prepared in manuscript.

WAR DIARY
or
INTELLIGENCE SUMMARY.
(Erase heading not required.)

Army Form C. 2118.

1st Royal Marine Battalion

Place	Date	Hour	Summary of Events and Information	Remarks and references to Appendices
FRONT LINE	18.8.16		Battn moved from Support to FRONT LINE, relieving the 2/R.M. Relief completed by 12:0 Noon. 'D' Coy Right, 'C' Coy Left in FIRING Line, 'B' Coy in MOROCCO NORTH, 'A' Coy ½ in GUMBOOT, ½ in MOROCCO SOUTH. Very quiet. 2nd Lieut H L Bennie & E L Platts joined Battn from 63rd (RN) Division Infantry Base Depot. Captain C H Bell South Lancashire Regt attached to Battn. No Casualties	FJC
FRONT LINE	19.8.16		Quiet. Lieut A. C. Donne RM & 1 O.R. proceeded to Lewis Gun School PERNES for a Course of Instruction. G.O.C. 63rd (RN) Division visited Sub-Section. Temp Lieut R. H. P. West to 63rd (RN) Division Infantry Base Depot for P B duty. No Casualties	FJC
FRONT LINE	20.8.16		Quiet during daylight. At 10.27 P.M. Enemy Rifle & Machine Gun fire became very brisk. At 10.30 P.M. our Artillery opened up a bombardment on Enemy salient opposite our line (M.26). At the same time Enemy position opposite ANGRES I & ANGRES II Sub Sections were attacked with Gas. Enemy replied with Heavy Artillery fire, Trench Mortars, & Rifle Grenades. Very little damage done to our trenches. Our patrols went out at about 11.45 P.M., & found Enemy very alert. They were unable to enter Enemy trenches. 2nd Lieut C. Rugg to Divisional Gas School for a Course of Instruction. 2nd Lieut F. W. Goldie & 10 O.R. rejoined Battn from Bomb School. 'D' Coy. 7th Battn Royal Fusiliers	FJC

T2134. Wt. W708–776. 500000. 4/15. Sir J. C. & S.

Instructions regarding War Diaries and Intelligence Summaries are contained in F. S. Regs., Part II. and the Staff Manual respectively. Title pages will be prepared in manuscript.

WAR DIARY
or
INTELLIGENCE SUMMARY.
(Erase heading not required.)

Army Form C. 2118.

1st Royal Marine Battalion

Place	Date	Hour	Summary of Events and Information	Remarks and references to Appendices
			Continued Fusiliers	
FRONT LINE	20	8 16	Attached to the Bath for instruction in FRONT LINE trenches.	JSL
FRONT LINE	21	8 16	Quiet. Lewis Guns relieved by Lewis Guns 2nd R.M. Battalion. On relief moved to Billets in BULLY GRENAY.	JSL
Bde Support	22	8 16	Battn relieved in FRONT LINE ANGRES II by 2nd R.M. Battn. On relief moved into Bde Support. Head Qrs, 'C' & 'D' Coys at BULLY GRENAY, 'A' Coy CORON D'AIX & CAP DE PONT, 'B' Coy in MECHANICS. One Casualty (wounded)	JSL
Bde Support	23	8 16	Usual Working Parties. Cleaning up, Baths. 2nd Lieut C. Rigg rejoined Battn from Divisional Gas School.	JSL
Bde Support	24	8 16	As for 23rd	JSL
Bde Support	25	8 16	As for 24th Captain C. H. Bell South Lancashire Regt left Battn for 18th Bde Head Quarters.	JSL
FRONT LINE	26	8 16	Battn moved from Support into FRONT LINE ANGRES II, relieving 2nd Battn R.M. Relief Completed by 11.30 A.M. Our Artillery fired about 100 rounds into Enemy wire. Our Trench Mortars were also busy Cutting Enemy wire. Enemy retaliation very feeble	JSL

Instructions regarding War Diaries and Intelligence Summaries are contained in F. S. Regs., Part II. and the Staff Manual respectively. Title pages will be prepared in manuscript.

WAR DIARY
or
INTELLIGENCE SUMMARY.
(Erase heading not required.)

Army Form C. 2118.

1st Royal Marine Battalion

Place	Date	Hour	Summary of Events and Information	Remarks and references to Appendices
FRONT LINE	24.8.16		Usual FRONT LINE routine. Fairly quiet. Our T Mortars bombarded Enemy wire for one hour. Enemy retaliated by firing about 20 minnies & a few Rifle Grenades. Casualties 3 O.R wounded HH	
FRONT LINE	28.8.16		Our 18 pounders & T. Mortars very busy cutting Enemy wire opposite this Sub-Section. Enemy retaliated with a few H.E. & minnies. Casualties two O.R. wounded. HH	
FRONT LINE	29.8.16		Our 18 pounders & T Mortars were active cutting wire (Enemy) opposite this Sub-section. Enemy made a feeble reply. A Test "Gas Helmet Alarm" was carried out. Lewis Guns relieved by L. Guns 2nd R.M. Bn. HH	
Bde Support	30.8.16		Battn was relieved in FRONT LINE by 2nd R.M. Battn. Relief was completed by 11.30 am. On relief Battn moved into Bde Support. Hd Qrs A & B Coys & Lewis Guns to BULLY GRENAY. "C" Coy to MECHANICS Trench, "D" Coy to CORON D'AIX & CAP DE PONT. HH	
Bde Support	31.8.16		Usual working parties. Cleaning up, & Baths. Lieut A C Donne rejoined Battn from Lewis Gun Course at PERNES. HH	

F J W Cartwright
Major R.M.L.I.
Comdg. 1st R.M. Battn.

T2134. Wt. W708—776. 500000. 4/15. Sir J. C. & S.

Confidential

Hd Qrs
1st Royal Marines
188th Bde 63rd (RN) Divn
1st October 1916

War Diary
of
1st Battalion Royal Marines
from
1st September 1916
to
30th September 1916

Hd Qrs
63rd (RN) Divn

F. J. W. Cartwright
Lieut Colonel RMLI
Comdg 1/Royal Marines

Volume IV (September) 1916.

Vol 4

1st Royal Marine Battalion

Army Form C. 2118.

Instructions regarding War Diaries and Intelligence Summaries are contained in F. S. Regs., Part II. and the Staff Manual respectively. Title pages will be prepared in manuscript.

WAR DIARY
or
INTELLIGENCE SUMMARY.
(Erase heading not required.)

Place	Date	Hour	Summary of Events and Information	Remarks and references to Appendices
BULLY GRENAY	1.9.16		Battalion in Brigade Support. Hd Qrs, 'A' + 'B' Coys, & Lewis Guns at BULLY GRENAY, 'C' Coy at MECHANICS TRENCH, 'D' Coy CORON D'AIX, & CAP DE PONT, Qr Master's Stores & 1st line Transport at BARLIN. No Casualties.	[initials]
—"—	2.9.16		In Brigade Support as above. No Casualties	[initials]
FRONT LINE ANGRES II Sub-Section	3.9.16		Battalion relieved 2nd R Marine Battn in Front Line trenches. 'C' Coy. 4th BEDFORD Regt were attached to this Unit. No Casualties	[initials]
As above	4.9.16		Very quiet in this Sub-Section. No Casualties	[initials]
As above	5.9.16		Usual Trench routine. 'C' Coy. 4th BEDFORDS rejoined their unit. No Casualties	[initials]
As above	6.9.16		Enemy Artillery a little more active than usual, but very little damage done. No Casualties.	[initials]
FOSSE 10.9 BULLY GRENAY	7.9.16	"	Battalion was relieved in Front line by 2nd Royal Marine Battn. Relief completed by 9.30 am. On relief Battn moved into Brigade Reserve, Head Qrs, C & D Coys + Lewis Guns at FOSSE 10, 'A' + 'B' Coys at BULLY GRENAY. Captain & Temp Major V.D. LOXLEY, Temp Lieut E. COHEN, Temp: Lieut T. W. PEARS, & Temp Lieut C. S. DESPREY, rejoined from Base ETAPLES. 10th Casualties 1 killed, & 3 slightly wounded (All Other ranks)	[initials]

T2134. Wt. W708—776. 500000. 4/15. Sir J. C. & S.

Instructions regarding War Diaries and Intelligence Summaries are contained in F. S. Regs., Part II. and the Staff Manual respectively. Title pages will be prepared in manuscript.

WAR DIARY
or
INTELLIGENCE SUMMARY.
(Erase heading not required.)

1st Royal Marine Battalion

Army Form C. 2118.

Place	Date	Hour	Summary of Events and Information	Remarks and references to Appendices
FOSSE 10, BULLY GRENAY	8.9.16		Brigade Reserve. No Casualties	[illegible]
AS Above	9.9.16		Brigade Reserve. No Casualties	[illegible]
AS Above	10.9.16		Brigade Reserve. Major F. J. W. CARTWRIGHT promoted to Lieut Colonel Temp 12. 8. 16. No Casualties	[illegible]
FRONT LINE ANGRES II	11.9.16		Battn relieved 2nd R.M. Battn in FRONT LINE. Relief completed by 10.30 Am. Temp 2nd Lieut D. A. PIPE transferred to 190th Brigade. No Casualties	[illegible]
AS Above	12.9.16		Our Artillery bombarded THOMPSONS CRATER. Results very satisfactory. No Casualties	[illegible]
AS Above	13.9.16		Ordinary F.L. routine. Temp Lieut A. C. DONNE to CLARQUES for a course of instruction in Trench mortars. No Casualties	[illegible]
AS Above	14.9.16		Very Quiet. Usual F.L. routine. No Casualties	[illegible]
FOSSE 10, BULLY GRENAY	15.9.16		Battn relieved in FRONT LINE by 2nd R.M. Battn; Relief completed by 11.0 Am. On relief Battn moved into Brigade Reserve. Head Qrs 'A' & 'B' Coys & Lewis Guns at FOSSE 10, 'C' & 'D' Coys at BULLY GRENAY. No Casualties	[illegible]
AS Above	16.9.16		Brigade Reserve. No Casualties	[illegible]
AS Above	17.9.16		Brigade Reserve. No Casualties	[illegible]
AS Above	18.9.16		Brigade Reserve. No Casualties	[illegible]

T2134. Wt. W708—776. 500000. 4/15. Sir J. C. & S.

Instructions regarding War Diaries and Intelligence Summaries are contained in F. S. Regs., Part II. and the Staff Manual respectively. Title pages will be prepared in manuscript.

WAR DIARY
or
INTELLIGENCE SUMMARY.
(Erase heading not required.)

1st Royal Marine Battalion

Army Form C. 2118.

Place	Date	Hour	Summary of Events and Information	Remarks and references to Appendices
HERSIN	19.9.16		Battn vacated billets at FOSSE 10, & BULLY GRENAY, & moved into Billets at HERSIN Move completed by 12.0 Noon. Temp Lieut & Temp Capt J. M. POUND, Temp 2nd Lieut S. J. H. PRYNNE & Temp 2nd Lieut T. O. CALLENDER, rejoined Battn. Capt POUND from Brigade Bomb School, 2nd Lieuts PRYNNE, & CALLENDER from "Dug Out" Party respectively.	
HERSIN, &	20.9.16		Battn moved by Route March from HERSIN, to DIEVAL. Time of departure 8.30 Am	
DIEVAL	"	"	Time of Arrival 1.30 P.M. The Corps Commander inspected the Battn as it marched by: at about 11.25 Am	
DIEVAL	21.9.16		Inspection of Clothing, equipment etc.	
DIEVAL	22.9.16		Battn Training. The Corps Commander presented medals to NCOs' & O. Men of The 63rd Division. The following Temp 2nd Lieuts promoted to Temp Lieuts on the dates specified against their names: John M POUND 3.4.16, N. B. WALKER 19.4.16, G. A. SULLIVAN 23.4.16, W. M. Hodding 12.8.16, B. A. SIMS 21.8.16, T. W. Pears 30.8.16, PETER DEWAR 30.8.16, J. E. CORNISH 19.4.16, C. S. DESPREZ 20.4.16, S. J. H. PRYNNE 28.4.16, T. O. CALLENDER 12.8.16, RONALD WEST 21.8.16, J. W. RICHARDS 30.8.16. Lieut (Temp) A G KYLE proceeded on 10 days leave to ENGLAND.	

Instructions regarding War Diaries and Intelligence Summaries are contained in F. S. Regs., Part II. and the Staff Manual respectively. Title pages will be prepared in manuscript.

WAR DIARY
or
INTELLIGENCE SUMMARY.
(Erase heading not required.)

1st Royal Marine Battalion

Army Form C. 2118.

Place	Date	Hour	Summary of Events and Information	Remarks and references to Appendices
DIEVAL	23.9.16		Battalion Training	[illegible]
As above	24.9.16		Battalion Training	[illegible]
As above	25.9.16		Battalion Training. Surgeon (Temp) F. B. SYKYN proceeded on 10 days leave to ENGLAND: Temp Lieut T. O. CALLENDER to Gas school for course of instruction	[illegible]
As Above	26.9.16		Battalion Training	[illegible]
As Above	27.9.16		Brigade Training: Lieut & Temp Capt L. F. NOURSE proceeded on 10 days leave to ENGLAND.	[illegible]
As Above	28.9.16		Brigade Training	[illegible]
As Above	29.9.16		Divisional Training. The Revd C. E. WHITEHEAD, joined this unit for duty. Temp 2nd Lieut H. E. BENNIE to Hospital (Sprained Ankle)	[illegible]
As above	30.9.16		The Battn took part in a Divisional Route march	[illegible]

F J W Cartwright

Lieut Colonel RMLI
Comdg 1/Royal Marines

T2134. Wt. W708—776. 500000. 4/15. Sir J. C. & S.

Confidential

Hd Qrs
1st Royal Marines
188th Bde, 63rd (RN) Dn
1st November 1916

63/Vol 5

War Diary
of
1st Battalion, Royal Marines
from
1st October 1916
to
31st October 1916.

Hd Qrs.
63rd (RN) Divn

F J W Cartwright
Lieut Colonel RMLI
Comdg 1/RM

Volume V (October) 1916

Instructions regarding War Diaries and Intelligence Summaries are contained in F. S. Regs., Part II. and the Staff Manual respectively. Title pages will be prepared in manuscript.

WAR DIARY
or
INTELLIGENCE SUMMARY.
(Erase heading not required.)

Army Form C. 2118.

Place	Date	Hour	Summary of Events and Information	Remarks and references to Appendices
DIEVAL	1.10.16		Medical Inspection & Divine Service. CM	
"	2.10.16		Company training on Brigade Training Area; Major H OZANNE & Captain C.LE.MUNTZ joined the Battn this day. CM	
"	3.10.16		Company training. Lieut L.G. Kyle rejoined from leave this day CM	
"	4.10.16		Battalion moved by route march to LIGNY ST FLOCHEL leaving at 8 a.m. A halt was made at MARQUAY for 7 hours. Battalion entrained at LIGNY ST FLOCHEL arriving at ACHEUX about 6 a.m. where it detrained & moved by route march to MAILLY-MAILLET where it went under canvas in MAILLEY WOOD.	CM
MAILLET WOOD	5.10.16		Company training.	CM
"	6.10.16		Company Training.	CM
"	7.10.16		Company Training. Surgeon Eykyn returned from leave this day	CM
"	8.10.16		Battalion left MAILLY WOOD & marched to VARENNES where it went into billets. The H.A.C Battn relieved 1/RM at MAILLY-WOOD	CM
VARENNES	9.10.16		Company training. A party of 6 Officers + 100 OR under Command of Major OZANNE attended instruction "In Communicating with Aircraft". The Battn Signal	

T2134. Wt. W708—776. 500000. 4/15. Sir J. C. & S.

WAR DIARY
or
INTELLIGENCE SUMMARY.
(Erase heading not required.)

Army Form C. 2118.

Instructions regarding War Diaries and Intelligence Summaries are contained in F. S. Regs., Part II. and the Staff Manual respectively. Title pages will be prepared in manuscript.

Place	Date	Hour	Summary of Events and Information	Remarks and references to Appendices
VARENNES	9.10.16		Staff also attended. In afternoon Battalion left Billets & marched to FORCEVILLE where it went into Billets. Captain L.F. NOURSE returned from leave the day. Lieut C.S. DESPREZ was attached to Prisoners of War Camp VARENNES	CA
FORCEVILLE	10.10.16		Company Training. Lt Col. CARTWRIGHT, Capt MUNTZ Maj. LOXLEY Lt WALKER Capt. BROWNE & Capt NOURSE visited the trench System E of COLINCHAMPS	
"	11.10.16		Company Training. One casualty in working party (O.R)	CA
"	12.10.16		Company Training. Major OZANNE Capts POUNDS, CLARKE, PINKERTON & HOARE visited trench System E of COLINCHAMPS.	
"	13.10.16		Company Training. 1/RM provided Funeral Guard of 200 O.R. at funeral of Captain (T. Major) E.P. SKETCHLEY R.M.L.I. at MILITARY CEMETERY FORCEVILLE, under command of Major H OZANNE.	CA
"	14.10.16		Company Training. Lt Col CARTWRIGHT, Capts MUNTZ, PINKERTON, BROWNE Lieuts RICHARDS & COULSON visited trench system near COLINCHAMPS	CA
"	15.10.16		Divine Service at FORCEVILLE. Battalion had hot baths at ACHEUX	CA
"	16.10.16		Company Training	CA
"	17.10.16		Company Training. Battalion vacated billets & moved by route march	

Instructions regarding War Diaries and Intelligence Summaries are contained in F. S. Regs., Part II. and the Staff Manual respectively. Title pages will be prepared in manuscript.

WAR DIARY
or
INTELLIGENCE SUMMARY.
(Erase heading not required.)

Army Form C. 2118.

Place	Date	Hour	Summary of Events and Information	Remarks and references to Appendices
FORCEVILLE	17.10.16		to HEDAUVILLE arriving 2pm where it went into Camp under Canvas (Tents & shelters)	CA
HEDAUVILLE	18.10.16		Company Training	CA
"	19-10-16		Company Training. Lt Col CARTWRIGHT, Captains MUNTZ, CLARKE, PINKERTON HOARE & BROWNE, Major LOXLEY & Lt RICHARDS reconnoitred trench system near HAMEL on N bank of RIVER ANCRE.	CA
"	20.10.16		Battalion moved by route march to ENGELBELMER where it went into Billets. Transport remained with QM. Stores at HEDAUVILLE.	CA
ENGELBELMER	21.10.16		In billets preparing for move to take over Section of the line tomorrow Lieut D.A. PIPE rejoined Battn from the 7th R. Fusiliers 190th Brigade, today	CA
	22.10.16		vacated billets & relieved the HOWE Battn in the line in the ~~BEAU~~ HAMEL Left SECTOR. Relief started at 6 am & was completed by 9.40 am. During the night we had several casualties Lieut T.W. PEARS wounded in the arm 1 OR killed & 1 OR wounded.	CA
FRONT LINE HAMEL Left	23-10-16		Trench routine. A great deal of work going on clearing up trenches & repairing them as they were constantly being blown in by enemy artillery & minenwerfer	

T2134. Wt. W708–776. 500000. 4/15. Sir J. C. & S.

Instructions regarding War Diaries and Intelligence Summaries are contained in F. S. Regs., Part II. and the Staff Manual respectively. Title pages will be prepared in manuscript.

WAR DIARY
or
INTELLIGENCE SUMMARY.
(Erase heading not required.)

Army Form C. 2118.

Place	Date	Hour	Summary of Events and Information	Remarks and references to Appendices
Front Line HAMEL L	23.10.16		Patrols went out & examined GERMAN wire. No Casualties.	
"	24.10.16		Trench routine, working parties at night digging new trench in advance of front line.	
"	25.10.16		Relieved in the line by HOWE Battn relief complete at 1.30 pm Battn returned to Billets in ENGELBELMER	
ENGELBELMER	26.10.16		In billets	
"	27.10.16		Vacated billets & relieved HOWE Battn in the line HAMEL Left Sector. Relief complete 3.10 pm. Sector very quiet.	
Front Line HAMEL L.	28.10.16		Trench routine. Some shelling with 5.9". The total equipment & rifles of 5 men was completely destroyed by shell bursting in a dugout. Capt Quill was confirmed as ADJUTANT 1/RM in D.R.O 27.10.16.	
"	29.10.16		Orders for 188th Bde to be relieved in the line by 190th Bde. Ordinary trench routine, working parties clearing up trenches & completing new trench. 5 OR Casualties wounded during night 29/30.	
"	30.10.16		Relieved by 4th BEDFORDSHIRE Regt. in the line & returned to Billets in ENGELBELMER arriving 3 pm. Relief was complete by 2 pm. Casualty one OR (shell shock	

T2134. Wt. W708–776. 500000. 4/15. Sir J. C. & S.

Instructions regarding War Diaries and Intelligence Summaries are contained in F. S. Regs., Part II. and the Staff Manual respectively. Title pages will be prepared in manuscript.

WAR DIARY
or
INTELLIGENCE SUMMARY.
(Erase heading not required.)

Army Form C. 2118.

Place	Date	Hour	Summary of Events and Information	Remarks and references to Appendices
ENGELBELMER	31.10.16		Vacated Billets & proceeded by route march to VARENNES leaving at 9.45 am & arriving at 11.45 am The Battalion went into Camp in HUTS	CM

T2134. Wt. W708-776. 500000. 4/15. Sir J. C. & S.

Vol 6

CONFIDENTIAL

1st Batt Royal Marines
188th Infntry Bgde
63rd (RN) Divn.

War Diary
of
1st Battn. Royal Marines
from
1st November
to
30th November

H.Q.
63rd (R.N.) Divn.

F W Cartwright
Lieut Col. RMLI
commndg 1st Batt. RM.

Volume VI November 1916.

Instructions regarding War Diaries and Intelligence Summaries are contained in F. S. Regs., Part II. and the Staff Manual respectively. Title pages will be prepared in manuscript.

WAR DIARY
or
INTELLIGENCE SUMMARY.
(Erase heading not required.)

Army Form C. 2118.

Place	Date	Hour	Summary of Events and Information	Remarks and references to Appendices
VARENNES	1.11.16		In huts - very muddy - working parties, cleaning camps & roads,	J Brand
—	2.11.16		large working parties on road. Battn. bathed at ACHEUX	
—	3.11.16		— — — — very wet - ground & roads very muddy	J Brand
—	4.11.16		— — — — Medical Inspection - under orders to move to PUCHVILLERS	J Brand
—	5.11.16		left VARENNES moved to PUCHVILLERS arrived 11.45am. Transport rejoined Battn from	
—			HEDAUVILLE	J Brand
PUCHVILLERS	6.11.16		orders recd. at 12 NOON to move at 1.45 pm to HEDAUVILLE, where we arrived at 5.25 pm in huts	
—	7.11.16		orders recd to relieve 10th Battn Dublin Fusiliers in HAMEL sector, where we marched in rain. Relief complete 2.15 pm. "W" (3 days previous to attack on German trench system)	J Brand
LINE	8.11.16		returned to ENGELBELMER relieved at 3pm. Killed. 1. O.R. In billets	
ENGELBELMER	9.11.16		vacated billets at 11.15 am & marched to VARENNES - in huts. T/Capt PINKERTON to Hosp. 2/Lieut COULSON - " -	J Brand
VARENNES	10.11.16		moved at 1pm & took over left HAMEL sector from NELSON Battn, being "W" day	J Brand
LINE	11.11.16		usual trench routine. "X" day for operations, which we are busy preparing for.	
—	12.11.16		moved up to Battle positions at 2.30 pm. "Y" day. Lieut. WALKER rejoined Battn from Hospital. Casualties. Capt Clarke wounded & about 30 O.R. killed & wounded	J Brand

T.134. Wt. W708-776. 500000. 4/15. Sir J. C. & S.

Instructions regarding War Diaries and Intelligence Summaries are contained in F. S. Regs., Part II. and the Staff Manual respectively. Title pages will be prepared in manuscript.

WAR DIARY
or
INTELLIGENCE SUMMARY.
(Erase heading not required.)

Army Form C. 2118.

Place	Date	Hour	Summary of Events and Information	Remarks and references to Appendices
LINE.	13.11.16		Battn was the left of the 188th Infty Bgde which attacked German trench system. It was in touch on left with 1/7 Gordon Highlanders. Following officers took part. Lieut. Col. F.J.W. CARTWRIGHT Major V.D. LOXLEY killed, Capt. C.LE.MUNTZ, wounded, Capt. H. HOARE killed, Capt. M.C. BROWNE, D.S.C. killed Capt. G.H. Sulivan, killed Capt. J.M. POUND missing. Lieut F.J. HANSON. killed. Lieut. A.G. KYLE, wounded Lieut. C. WATKINS, wounded. Lieut. A.C. DONNE, wounded Lieut E. COHEN wounded, Lieut. N.B. WALKER, wounded Lieut. H.B. VAN PRAAGH, Lieut. W.M. HODDING, wounded. Lieut. P. DEWAR wounded, 2Lieut. F. GOLDIE wounded. 2Lieut E.L. PLATTS wounded, 2nd Lieut C.W. MARTIN, killed Lieut J.W. RICHARDS, missing 2Lieut H.E.R. UPHAM missing Surgn. F.B. EYKYN - wounded.	
			The attack commenced on the opening of our barrage at 5.45 am. when Battn advanced in 4 waves - one platoon of each company in a wave. There was a very thick mist. Every Company Commander was killed before crossing German front line. Enemy trenches were practically obliterated by our artillery. NO MAN'S LAND & ground between various German lines, as far as slope down to STATION ROAD was pitted with shell holes, deep & very muddy. Ground crossed by this Battn was particularly muddy which made advance difficult. Within a minute of our barrage starting, Enemy replied with artillery barrage on Support Lines and	

and

Instructions regarding War Diaries and Intelligence Summaries are contained in F. S. Regs., Part II. and the Staff Manual respectively. Title pages will be prepared in manuscript.

WAR DIARY
or
INTELLIGENCE SUMMARY.
(Erase heading not required.)

Army Form C. 2118.

Place	Date	Hour	Summary of Events and Information	Remarks and references to Appendices
			and	
LINE.	13.11.16		No Mans Land, where they also opened a heavy Machine Gun fire. It is estimated that at least 50% of casualties occurred between No Mans Land & German 1st Line. Between 2nd & 3rd Line, ground was swept with M.G. fire. Here also were heavy casualties. Isolated parties of this Battn followed the barrage as far as YELLOW LINE & got in touch with HAC on right. They were not however sufficiently strong to ~~get~~ close gap between H.A.C. & Battn on left. Remnant of this Battn held dotted BLUE LINE during night 13/14th, in partially constructed trench W. of STATION Rd. Touch was maintained during night with 4th Gordon Highlanders on left	
LINE.	14.11.16	6 AM.	Battn advanced & dug in to E of STATION ROAD. During course of day various small scattered parties rejoined. Capt L.F. NOURSE & 80 reinforcements ~~rejoined~~ joined Battn about 8 pm. Position shelled intermittently thro' day & night	
LINE.	15.11.16		Still being shelled. Battn was withdrawn at 2pm. marched to HEDAUVILLE by 6.30pm ~~route march~~. Moved from there to PUCHVILLERS by lorries about 11.30 pm.	
			Battn advanced 490 strong & returned 138 strong having had 47 men killed, 210 wounded & 85 missing. Of the *22 officers who took part only 2 returned – 6 being killed	22
			* 11 wounded & 3 missing.	11

T.134. Wt. W708–776. 500000. 4/15. Sir J. C. & S.

Instructions regarding War Diaries and Intelligence Summaries are contained in F. S. Regs., Part II. and the Staff Manual respectively. Title pages will be prepared in manuscript.

WAR DIARY
or
INTELLIGENCE SUMMARY.
(Erase heading not required.)

Army Form C. 2118.

Place	Date	Hour	Summary of Events and Information	Remarks and references to Appendices
DUCHVILLERS	16.11.16		Resting + cleaning. clear fine day	
–	17.11.16		vacated billets + marched to GEZAINCOURT. Capt MUNTZ – died of wounds viewed by Divl. Genl	
GEZAINCOURT	18.11.16		– – – – BERNAVILLE	
BERNAVILLE	19.11.16		resting + cleaning – 40 reinforcements joined Battn. very wet.	
–	20.11.16		weather finer *addressed by Divl. Gen. Major Gen. SHUTE CB Surgt. BLACKWELL RN joined Battn.	*addressed
–	21.11.16		vacated billets + marched to CRAMONT. billeting accommodation very limited. fine.	
CRAMONT	22.11.16		– – – – – FROYELLES	
FROYELLES	23.11.16		– – – – – LE.TITRE	
LE TITRE	24.11.16		– – – – – our destination MORLAY – ground very low + marshy raining heavily – 3 companies billetted at PONTHOILE – HQ + other company MORLAY.	
MORLAY	25.11.16		still raining slightly. very cold 225 reinforcements arrived at night	
–	26.11.16		Fine + frosty. Battn started training. hours 9 – 12 am 2 – 3 pm	
–	27.11.16		– – Battn training continued. hours altered from 9 – 12.30. afternoons being devoted to sports.	
	28.11.16		– – – – – –	
	29.11.16		– – –	
	30.11.16		– – – – – –	

T2134. Wt. W708–776. 500000. 4/15. Sir J. C. & S.

Confidential

Vol 7

H.Q. 1st Royal Marine (Battn
188th Infty Bgde. 63rd (RN) Dn
1st Jan. 1917.

War Diary
of
1st. Royal Marine Battn
from
1st Dec. 1916 to 31st Dec 1916

VOL. VII

H.Qrs
63rd (RN) Divn.

F J W Cartwright
Lieut. Col. RMLI
Commdg 1st RM Battn

Instructions regarding War Diaries and Intelligence Summaries are contained in F. S. Regs., Part II. and the Staff Manual respectively. Title pages will be prepared in manuscript.

WAR DIARY
or
INTELLIGENCE SUMMARY.
(Erase heading not required.)

Army Form C. 2118.

Place	Date	Hour	Summary of Events and Information	Remarks and references to Appendices
MORLAY.	1.12.16		Coy Training – Digging Brigade Practice trenches	J. Brand
–	2.12.16		– – wet day	
–	3.12.16		Divine Service + muster of kits	
–	4.12.16		Coy Training. 2nd Lieuts DAPPE + C. RUGG promoted Lieut (10.11.16) (25.11.16) long list of NCOs promoted to complete establishment	J. Brand
–	5.12.16		Lt. Col. CARTWRIGHT on leave – Major OZANNE assumed command of Batt: Coy Training.	
–	6.12.16		Battn route march. Capt PINKERTON to leave.	J. Brand
–	7.12.16		Coy Training 53 OR joined Battn from Base	
–	8.12.16		Battn – wet + cold.	
–	9.12.16		Coy –	J. Brand
–	10.12.16		Divine Service. Lieut DONNE to leave.	
–	11.12.16		2 subaltern off + 151 OR joined Battn from Base.	
–	12.12.16		Coy + Battn Training	J. Brand
–	13.12.16		Battn moved by route march from MORLAY to VRON into billets.	
VRON	14.12.16		Battn Training. Battn arias Bombing Competition + cross country run. 1 Capt + 11 subaltern officers joined Battn from Base (England)	J. Brand

T.134. Wt. W708–776. 500000. 4/15. Sir J. C. & S.

Instructions regarding War Diaries and Intelligence Summaries are contained in F. S. Regs., Part II. and the Staff Manual respectively. Title pages will be prepared in manuscript.

WAR DIARY
or
INTELLIGENCE SUMMARY.
(Erase heading not required.)

Army Form C. 2118.

Place	Date	Hour	Summary of Events and Information	Remarks and references to Appendices
VRON	15.12.16		Battn Training – Improvement of billets commenced – Bathing arrangements (commenced	[signature]
–	16.12.16		– – Sergt. BLACKWELL & Lieut. H. VAN PRAAGH to leave – Sports in afternoon.	
–	17.12.16		Divine Service. Lt Col. CARTWRIGHT from leave – 3. O.R. from Base. – –	[signature]
–	18.12.16		Battn Training. Assessment of character commenced. Digging trenches at VERCOURT.	
–	19.12.16		– – Lieut PEARSON to 5th Army School Sports in afternoon	[signature]
–	20.12.16		Battn route march – –	
–	21.12.16		Battn Training – visit by Army Commander. – – –	
–	22.12.16		Battn – Lieut DONNE & Rev. WHITEHEAD from leave – – – –	[signature]
–	23.12.16		Battn –	
–	24.12.16		Divine Service. following awards of Military Medal in connection with operations N of ANCRE	[signature]
–	25.12.16		– – Sports, football etc in afternoon (Cpl. 8382 A/Sgt HESELTON. Cpl. 438(S) Pte WYATT / Cpl. 8107 A/Sgt GANNON. Pty 1046(S) Pte J. SMITH. / 17487 Pte H. GODFREY. Cpl. 17669 Pte E. GILL.	
–	26.12.16		Battn Training – – –	
–	27.12.16		– – practice attack on Bgde trenches VERCOURT.	[signature]
–	28.12.16		– – Lieut. H. VAN PRAAGH from leave.	
–	29.12.16		– –	
–	30.12.16		– –	
–	31.12.16		Divine Service	

T.134. Wt. W708–776. 500000. 4/15. Sir J. C. & S.

Confidential.

H.Q. 1st Royal Marine Battalion
188th Inf. Bde
63rd Div.
2nd Feb. 1917.

908

War Diary
of
1st Royal Marine Battalion.
from
1st January 1917 to 31st January 1917.

To
The A.G's. Office
3rd Echelon.

F J W Cartwright
Lt. Col. Cmdg
1st R.M. Battalion.

Volume. 8.

Instructions regarding War Diaries and Intelligence Summaries are contained in F. S. Regs., Part II. and the Staff Manual respectively. Title pages will be prepared in manuscript.

WAR DIARY
or
INTELLIGENCE SUMMARY.
(Erase heading not required.)

Army Form C. 2118.

1st Royal Marine Battalion

Place	Date	Hour	Summary of Events and Information	Remarks and references to Appendices
VRON	1.1.17.	-	Battalion carried out attack practice in trenches E. of VERCOURT.	E/H
"	2.1.17.		Half Officers of Battalion attended a Field Engineering Course at RUE, in forenoon. In afternoon all Officers attended a meeting presided over by the Corps Commander at NOUVION. 2nd Lt. Lee proceeded to ARRY for L.T.M. Course. Company training. Major F.B.W. Wellesley. West Riding Regt. joined Battn.	E/H
"	3.1.17.		2nd Lt. Balcombe reported for Bayonet Fighting Course at Bde. Hq. VRON. Company training.	E/H
"	4.1.17.	8.0am to 1.30pm	Brigade Attack practice carried out in trenches E. of VERCOURT.	E/H
"	5.1.17.		Battalion Training. Half Officers of Battalion attended a Field Engineering Course at RUE	E/H
"	6.1.17.		Company Training. All officers attended a demonstration by Special Platoon in trenches E. of VERCOURT	E/H
"	7.1.17.		Divine Service	E/H
"	8.1.17.		2nd Lt. Savage proceeded on Gas Course. Half Officers of Battalion attended a Field Engineering Course at RUE. Company Training.	E/H
"	9.1.17.		Half Officers of Battalion attended Field Engineering Course at RUE. Remainder attended a lecture on Aeroplane photographs in the afternoon. Battalion Training.	E/H
"	10.1.17.		Battalion employed filling in all practise trenches.	E/H
"	11.1.17.		Transport inspected by Divisional Commander	E/H

T.134. Wt. W708-776. 500000. 4/15. Sir J. C. & S.

Instructions regarding War Diaries and Intelligence Summaries are contained in F. S. Regs., Part II. and the Staff Manual respectively. Title pages will be prepared in manuscript.

WAR DIARY
or
INTELLIGENCE SUMMARY.
(Erase heading not required.)

Army Form C. 2118.

1st Royal Marine Battalion

Place	Date	Hour	Summary of Events and Information	Remarks and references to Appendices
VRON	12.1.17.		Battalion clearing up billets, returning stores etc. 2nd Lt. Fielding proceeded to LE TOUQUET L.G. Course.	[initials]
— " —	13.1.17.		Battalion vacated billets at VRON, and moved by Route March to SAILLY-BRAY via. VRON, BERNAY, + NOUVION.	[initials]
SAILLYBRAY	14.1.17.		Battalion vacated billets at SAILLYBRAY, and moved by route march to DOMVAST. via. LE TITRE, and cross roads W. of D in DOMVAST.	[initials]
DOMVAST	15.1.17.		Battalion vacated billets at DOMVAST. and moved by route march to BOIS BERQUES via. BRAILLY, AGENVILLE, road junction just west of P in PROUVILLE, BERNAVILLE.	[initials]
BOIS BERQUES. — " —	16.1.17.		Battalion rested. Lieutenants J. E. Cornish and H. W. Hall joined Battalion	
— " —	17.1.17		Battalion vacated billets at BOIS BERQUES., and moved by route march to BEAUQUESNE via. road junction N. end of OUTRE BOIS, on the N side of River AUTHIE. recrossing river at HEM. BRELET, and main road immediately E. of DOULENS. CITADEL – LE BON AIR. – HULEUX – TERRA MESNIL.	[initials]
BEAUQUESNE.	18.1.17.		2 Platoons Nos. 6 + 8, Lieut Robinson (in command) and 2nd Lt. Okell, attached to the 2nd Royal Marines for Special duty. Remainder of Battalion billeted. 2nd Lt Fielding to hospital	[initials]
— " —	19.1.17.		Battalion billeted.	[initials]
— " —	20.1.17.		Battalion vacated billets at BEAUQUESNE, and moved by bus to ENGLEBELMER. via. ARQUEVES, LEALVILLERS, VARENNES, HEDAUVILLE.	[initials]

Instructions regarding War Diaries and Intelligence Summaries are contained in F. S. Regs., Part II. and the Staff Manual respectively. Title pages will be prepared in manuscript.

WAR DIARY
or
INTELLIGENCE SUMMARY.
(Erase heading not required.)

Army Form C. 2118.

1st Royal Marine Battalion

Place	Date	Hour	Summary of Events and Information	Remarks and references to Appendices
	January.		21st Lieut R. West. returned from leave.	FJWC
			22nd Lieut R. West. proceeded to Div. School Nouvion for course of instruction. Lieut. Champness joined Battalion	FJWC
ENGLEBELMER.	21st – 24th		~~Fatigues~~ Various large working parties. C.O. & Adjutant visited the Sector to be taken over on 23rd. One Officer and one N.C.O. per Company moved into the line on 24th and remained.	FJWC
	25th		1st Royal Marines relieved the 2nd Royal Marines in the line in the St. PIERRE DIVION Sector. 1st line D. Coy. - CANAL and FERDAN Trench. 2nd line A Coy. - HANSA trench. - 3rd line (Reserve) - B + C Companies - in Tunnel. Relief completed 7.0 pm. Casualty Ch 878.S. Pte. C. Burton wounded.	FJWC
	27th		Casualties - Ch/976.S. Pte. J. Storey and Ch/967.S. Pte. A. Younger. - Killed. C/61.S. H. Morley Ch/12429. R. Adams - wounded. Internal relief carried out. - C company relieved D Company in CANAL and FERDAN line B. company will relieve A company in HANSA line	FJWC
	28th		Casualty. Ply. 728'S. Pte. R. Richards. wounded. Lieut. H. Lyon proceeded for course to 5th Army School. DOMAT-EN-PONTHIEU	FJWC
	29th		Internal relief carried out. A Company relieved C Company in CANAL and FERDAN line D Company relieved B Coy in HANSA line. Patrols located two Hostile posts in Battery Valley.	FJWC
	30.		Casualty. A.Coy. Ch. 1510 Pte. W. Pye. wounded	
	31st		2nd Royal Marines relieved the 1st Royal Marines 1st R.M. billeted as follows:- H.Q. C Company (less one platoon) and D Coy billeted ENGLEBELMER. 1 Platoon "C" Coy billeted with 1st Field Ambulance. N. end of AVELUY WOOD. "A" company ~~to~~ + B Company ~~in~~ dugouts in THIEPVAL WOOD.	FJWC

F J W Cartwright
Lt. Col. Cmdg. 1st R.M.

T.134. Wt. W708–776. 500000. 4/15. Sir J. C. & S.

Confidential.

Head Quarters.

1st Battalion Royal Marines

2nd March. 1917.

4029

War Diary

of

1st Battalion. Royal Marines.

from.

1st February 1917.

to

28th February 1917.

F. J. W. Cartwright

Lt. Col. R.M.L.I.

Cmdg. 1st Royal Marines

To
The A.G.s Office
3rd Echelon.

Volume IX.

Instructions regarding War Diaries and Intelligence Summaries are contained in F. S. Regs., Part II. and the Staff Manual respectively. Title pages will be prepared in manuscript.

WAR DIARY
or
~~INTELLIGENCE SUMMARY.~~
(*Erase heading not required.*)

Army Form C. 2118.

1st R.M. Battalion

Place	Date	Hour	Summary of Events and Information	Remarks and references to Appendices
	1.2.17			
ENGLEBELMER.			1st R.M. billeted as follows:- H.Q. C Company (less one platoon) and D Company billeted in ENGLEBELMER; one platoon billeted with 1st Field Ambulance, N. of AVELUY wood; A and B Companies & in dugouts in THIEPVAL WOOD	S/H
	2.2.17		——— . ——— . Working Parties found by the Battalion.	S/H
	3.2.17		——— " ——— Working Parties found by the Battalion	S/H
	4.2.17		Divine Service. Capt. Burton, proceeded on leave to England.	S/H
	5.2.17		Labour Company formed. 1 Platoon furnished by 1st R.M. consisting of Lt Cornish (2nd in command of Company) and 26 N.C.O. and men. Lt Hall proceeded on Gas Course.	S/H S/H
	6.2.17		Lieut. Hall procedede on Gas Course to FORCEVILLE. Working parties and Companies at training	S/H
	7.2.17		Company training.	
	8.2.17		Battalion Hd Qrs, C and D Companies vacated billets at ENGLEBELMER B and C companies relieved 2nd R.M in front and support lines, Eastern end of GRANDCOURT.	S/H
	9.2.17		A company relieved company of 2nd R.M.s occupying O.G.I. CANAL, + FERDAN. D company relieved company of 2nd R.M.s occupying HANSA. Lt Hall returned from Gas Course.	S/H.

T.134. Wt. W703-776. 500000. 4/15. Sir J. C. & S.

Instructions regarding War Diaries and Intelligence Summaries are contained in F. S. Regs., Part II. and the Staff Manual respectively. Title pages will be prepared in manuscript.

WAR DIARY
or
~~INTELLIGENCE~~ SUMMARY.
(Erase heading not required.)

Army Form C. 2118.

1st R.M. Battalion

Place	Date	Hour	Summary of Events and Information	Remarks and references to Appendices
1917				
~~9.2.17.~~	9.2.17.		B and C Companies relieved by 12th Middlesex (2 Companies) in GRANDCOURT, — marching to huts in MARTINSART	S/H
	10.2.17		Battalion Head Quarters, A + D Companies, vacated CHALK PALACE, FERDAN + HANSA, and moved by route march to huts in MARTINSART	S/H
	11.2.17.		C.O. visited new line N. of ANCRE. Battalion employed large working parties.	S/H
	12.2.17		Battalion found large working parties. One officer per company proceeded to new line N. of ANCRE.	S/H
	13.2.17		Battalion found large working parties. Casualties 4 wounded	S/H
	14.2.17.		The 1st Royal Marines relieved the 10th Royal Dublin Fusiliers in the RIVER TRENCH SECTOR, N. of GRANDCOURT. B + D Companies Hd. Qrs in PUSIEUX TRENCH. Battalion Hd Qrs. PUSIEUX ROAD. Captn. Nourse to 2nd Field Ambulance (Influenza) - Casualties 2 killed - 1 offr 2nd Lt. Lee and 9 other Ranks wounded.	S/H
	15.2.17.		Relief completed 3.0 am Casualties 6 killed - 3 Missing - 9 wounded.	S/H
	16.2.17.		Battalion Hd. Qrs moved forward to PUSIEUX Trench. Battalion lined up for attack at 10.0 pm. Objective SUNKEN ROAD - L32c 91 to R Ca 26 including two strong Points, that on the right being known as the PIMPLE. Posts had to be established 50 yards beyond the Road.	S/H

T.134. Wt. W708-776. 500000. 4/15. Sir J. C. & S.

Instructions regarding War Diaries and Intelligence Summaries are contained in F. S. Regs., Part II. and the Staff Manual respectively. Title Pages will be prepared in manuscript.

WAR DIARY
or
INTELLIGENCE SUMMARY
(Erase heading not required.)

Army Form C. 2118

1st Royal Marine Battalion

Place	Date	Hour	Summary of Events and Information	Remarks and references to Appendices
	16.2.17		HOWE Battalion to attack on our right – 2nd R.M. Battalion held ARTILLERY ALLEY and protected left flank. ANSON Battalion held position R2d75 – R3c37 – R3c63. The following officers were with the Battalion in the attack. Lieut. Col. F.J.W. Cartwright. D.S.O, Major H. Ozanne (wounded) Major F.H.B Wellesley. West Riding Regiment (wounded) Captain S.J. Hutchesson, Captain J. Pearson, Lieut. H.W.R. Hall, Lieut. A.C. Donne (wounded), Lieut. L.W. Robinson (killed), 2nd Lieut. A.A. Okell (killed) 2nd Lieut. F. Savage (killed) 2nd Lieut. E. Sanderson (wounded), 2nd Lieut. C.R. Burton (killed), 2nd Lieut C.L. Rugg (severely wounded), Lieutenant E.G. Coulson (killed), 2nd Lt. W.C. Gudlestone (wounded). Lieutenant R.E. Champness, Lieutenant F.W.A. Perry (killed), 2nd Lieut. H.C. Brown (killed), Surgeon Unthank. R.N.	E/H
	17.2.17		Advance commenced at 5.45 am. on barrage opening. Our dispositions were, from right to left D.B.C.A, companies were extended at 2 paces interval, + in two waves at 20 paces distance. The lines were subjected to heavy bombardment by 77 mm. at about 5.0 am. necessitating a call for retaliation by our Artillery. Reports were received at 6.40 am to effect that the battalion	

1875 Wt. W593/826 1,000,000 4/15 J.B.C. & A. A.D.S.S./Forms/C. 2118.

Instructions regarding War Diaries and Intelligence Summaries are contained in F. S. Regs., Part II. and the Staff Manual respectively. Title pages will be prepared in manuscript.

WAR DIARY
or
INTELLIGENCE SUMMARY.
(*Erase heading not required.*)

Army Form C. 2118.

1st R.M. Battalion

Place	Date	Hour	Summary of Events and Information	Remarks and references to Appendices
			had gained their objective, and that the PIMPLE had been captured. 102 Prisoners were taken, 1-77 mm gun, & 2 machine guns were	
	18.2.17.		captured. The enemy counter attacked on three occasions. On one occasion taking advantage of thick mist, he counter attacked, without artillery preparation, 2 battalions strong, on 1½ mile frontage. S.O.S. message was sent, the artillery replying with great promptitude, causing many casualties. The battalion on the left, turned and fled, and was almost immediately followed by the right battalion. The line from Battalion Hd Qrs to front line had only just been repaired when S.O.S. was asked for. Total casualties suffered by the Battalion in the attack, capture and consolidation of the objective - SUNKEN ROAD - Officers - 7 killed - 6 wounded. Other ranks - 57 killed - 193 wounded - 27 missing.	JH
	19.2.17		1st R.M. Battalion relieved in the line during the night of the 18th/19th Feb. by 2nd R.M. Battalion. Relief completed 7.0 am. Companies moving independently to old German 2nd and 3rd lines - Q 18 a 30 - 1500 yards SSE of BEAUMONT HAMEL. Major Ozanne to Field Ambulance	JH
	20.2.17		Captain Pearson, Lieutenant Champness, 2nd Lt. Hall evacuated to Field Ambulance	JH

T.134. Wt. W708-776. 500000. 4/15. Sir J. C. & S.

Instructions regarding War Diaries and Intelligence Summaries are contained in F. S. Regs., Part II. and the Staff Manual respectively. Title pages will be prepared in manuscript.

WAR DIARY
or
INTELLIGENCE SUMMARY.
(*Erase heading not required.*)

Army Form C. 2118.

1st R.M. Battalion

Place	Date	Hour	Summary of Events and Information	Remarks and references to Appendices
ENGLEBELMER	21.2.17		1st Royal Marines relieved by the 10th Bn Royal Dublin Fusiliers. Relief completed 3.0pm. Battalion moved by route march to ENGLEBELMER via: HAMEL – MESNIL – MARTINSART. The Battalion was met in MARTINSART by the ~~band of the~~ DEAL, R.M.L.I. Band, + played into billets.	AH
"	22.2.17		Battalion re organising. Following officers joined the Battalion. Lieut. Platts, 2nd Lts. A.S.R. Perry, O.A. Roberts, L.G. Evans, C.C.G. Poe, B.G. Evanson, J.V. Atkinson, J. Fielding, J.W. Thomas, F.S. Marsh, L. Lees and 94 other ranks — Major H.O. Ozanne rejoined unit from 45th C.C.S.	AH
"	23.2.17		Battalion found working parties. 2nd Lts. W.S. Llewelyn, + H.A. Carruthers joined the Battalion and 12 other ranks	AH
"	24.2.17		Battalion reorganising and small working parties found	AH
"	25.2.17		Battalion re organising and small working parties found	AH
"	26.2.17		Battalion re organising and small working parties found. 2nd Lt. Kenny and burial Party sent up to SUNKEN ROAD – 2nd Lts. Robinson and Okell, +11 O.R. buried	AH
"	27.2.17		2nd Lt. Fielding and burial party sent up to SUNKEN-ROAD: 21 N.C.Os + men buried	AH
"	28.2.17		Battalion vacated billets at ENGLEBELMER and moved by route march to BRUCE HUTS (W.16.a.3.2), 500 yards W. of AVELUY Bridge.	AH

F.J.W. Cartwright
Lt. Col. Cmdg.
1st Royal Marine Battalion

T.131. Wt. W708–776. 500000. 4/15. Sir J. C. & S.

"Confidential"

Vol 10

Headquarters
1st Bn Royal Marines L.I.

Volume X

War Diary
of
1st Battn Royal Marine Light Infantry
from
1st March 1917
to
31st March 1917

F. J. W. Cartwright
Lieut. Colonel
Commanding 1st R.M.L.I.

To the A.G's Office
3rd Echelon

Instructions regarding War Diaries and Intelligence Summaries are contained in F. S. Regs., Part II. and the Staff Manual respectively. Title Pages will be prepared in manuscript.

WAR DIARY
or
INTELLIGENCE SUMMARY
(Erase heading not required.)

Army Form C. 2118

Place	Date	Hour	Summary of Events and Information	Remarks and references to Appendices
Bruce Huts AVELOY	1.3.17		Large Working Parties found for Road repairing & Saw Mills AVELOY WOOD. Signallers, Lewis Gunners, Bombers, snipers + Band to Instruction. HO.	
— " —	2.3.17		T/Capt Pearson from Div. Rest Station	
			T/Lieut Champness from C.C.S.	
			Drills + Working Parties as for 1st 3.17 HO.	
— " —	3.3.17		T/2nd Lieut H.T. Holmes from Base Depot. 26 O.R. joined Bn from Base Depot	
			Drills + Working Parties as above HO.	
— " —	4.3.17		~~Drills~~ + Working Parties as above HO.	
— " —	5.3.17		Major H. Ozanne to leave. Drills + Working Parties as above. HO.	
— " —	6.3.17		Drills + W.P. as above HO.	
— " —	7.3.17		T/Lt. John Pearson promoted T/Captain to date 27.2.17.	
			T/Capt. A. Nourse to England sick. struck off strength 25.2.17. HO.	
			Drills + W.P. as above.	
— " —	8.3.17		Drills + W.P. as above. HO.	
— " —	9.3.17		Drills + W.P. as above HO.	
— " —	10.3.17		13 O.R. joined Bn from Base Depot. Drills + W.P. as above. HO.	
— " —	11.3.17		Major H. Ozanne awarded D.S.O.	
			T/Capt. J. Pearson awarded Military Cross. 12 O.Rs. awarded Military Medal. HO.	
			W.P. as above	
— " —	12.3.17		Drills + working Parties as above HO.	

Instructions regarding War Diaries and Intelligence Summaries are contained in F. S. Regs., Part II. and the Staff Manual respectively. Title Pages will be prepared in manuscript.

WAR DIARY
or
INTELLIGENCE SUMMARY
(Erase heading not required.)

Army Form C. 2118

Place	Date	Hour	Summary of Events and Information	Remarks and references to Appendices
BRUCE HUTS	13.3.17		Drills and W. P. as above. HO.	
AVELOY	14.3.17		T/Lieut D. W. R. Hall to England sick. Struck off strength 2. 3. 17.	
			18 O.Rs joined Batt: from Base Depot. Drills & W. P. as above HO.	
—"—	15.3.17		T/Lt. R. E. Champness to 1st F.A. Drills & W. P. as above. HO.	
—"—	16.3.17		Drills & W. P. as above. HO.	
—"—	17.3.17		Major H. Ozanne from leave. Drills & W. P. as above. HO.	
—"—	18.3.17		T/Lt. J. E. Cornish from labour Company. &	
			T/Lt. R. E. Champness transferred from 1/F.A. to 49th C.C.S.	
			2nd Lt. H. A. Carruthers from 2nd F.A. HO.	
—"—	19.3.17		Lt. Colonel F. J. W. Cartwright D.S.O. to leave	
			Major H. Ozanne D.S.O. assumed command of Battalion.	
			12 O. R. joined Bn. from Base Depot.	
			Battalion left BRUCE HUTS 8.50 am & proceeded by Route March to HERRISART HO.	
HERRISART	20.3.17		Batt: left HERRISART 8.15 a.m. & proceeded by Route March to GEZAINCOURT HO.	
GEZAINCOURT	21.3.17		Batt: left GEZAINCOURT 10.7 a.m. & proceeded by route march to BOURET-SUR -CANACHE. HO.	
BOURET	22.3.17		Batt: left BOURET at 10.10 am & proceeded by route march to CROISETTE HO. 16 O.R. joined Batt: from Base Depot.	
CROISETTE	24.3.17		Batt left CROISETTE at 8.50 a.m. & proceeded by route march to SAINS-LES-PERNES HO.	
SAINS-LES-PERNES	25.3.17		Batt: left SAINS-LES-PERNES at 8.20 a.m. & proceeded by route march to ECQUEDECQUES. HO.	
ECQUEDEQUES	26.3.17		Batt: left ECQUEDEQUES at 9.30 am & proceeded by route march to CALONNE-SUR-LYS HO. Lt. N. I. Lyon to leave.	

1875 Wt. W593/826 1,000,000 4/15 J.B.C. & A. A.D.S.S./Forms/C. 2118.

Army Form C. 2118

Instructions regarding War Diaries and Intelligence Summaries are contained in F. S. Regs., Part II. and the Staff Manual respectively. Title Pages will be prepared in manuscript.

WAR DIARY
or
INTELLIGENCE SUMMARY
(Erase heading not required.)

Place	Date	Hour	Summary of Events and Information	Remarks and references to Appendices
CALONNE-SUR-LYS	27.3.17		Battⁿ left CALONNE at 9·15 a.m and proceeded by route march to HESDIGNEUL	HO
HESDIGNEUL	28.3.17		8 O.Rs joined Battⁿ from Base Depot. HO	
HESDIGN-EUL	29.3.17		Battⁿ left HESDIGNEUL and proceeded by Route March to LABOURSE HO Lieut. Colonel Cartwright D.S.O. from leave Capt. E.J. Huskisson to 2nd F.A.	
LABOURSE	30.3.17		Battⁿ training commenced. Battⁿ at six hours notice to move into the line	HO
			33 O.Rs. joined Battⁿ from Base Depot. Capt. E.J. Huskisson from 2nd F.A. to No 7 Gen. Hosp.	HO
— " —	31.3.17		Inf. training continued. 2nd Lt. B.G. Evanson to 1st F.A. HO	

F J W Cartwright
Lieut Colonel
Commanding 1st R.M.L.I.

1875 Wt. W593/826 1,000,000 4/15 J.B.C. & A. A.D.S.S./Forms/C. 2118.

<u>Confidential</u>

H.Q.
1st Battn R.M.L.I.

<u>Volume XI</u>

War Diary
of
1st Bn. Royal Marine Light Infantry
from
1st April 1917
to
30 April 1917

To A.G's office
3rd Echelon

H. Ozanne
Major RMLI
Commdg. 1st Bn.
Royal Marine L.I.

A.F.C. 2118.

WAR DIARY.

PLACE.	DATE.	HOUR.	SUMMARY OF EVENTS AND INFORMATION.	REMARKS AND REFERENCES TO APPENDICES.
LA BOURSE	1917 1st April.		Company training carried out. Captain A.E.H. Read. RAMC. taken on Battalion strength vice. Surgeon Unthank to England.	S/H
—.—	2nd April.		Infantry training continued.	S/H
—.—	3rd April		Infantry training continued.	S/H
—.—	4th April		Infantry training continued	S/H
—.—	5th April.		Infantry training continued. Orders received to relieve a Battalion of the 17th Infantry Brigade in the Line. Advanced parties of 1 N.C.O. and 1 officer [A] Battalion company sent up. Captain S/ Huskisson rejoined Battalion from No 7 Hospital	S/H
—.—	6th April		Battalion cleaning up billets, & making preparations for moving into the line. Battalion came under orders of G.O.C. 24th Division at 6.0 pm.	S/H
—.—	7th April		Battalion vacated billets at LA BOURSE, and moved into the line relieving the 12th Bn Royal Fusiliers, in the ANGRES II Sector. D. B, & A Companies in the Front line, C Company in Support, Battalion Hd Qrs in MECHANICS trench. 8th Buffs held the line on our right, East Surreys on our left. Platoon guides met Platoons at BULLY GRENAY at 3.0pm. relief completed 8.0 pm. Lieutenant H. B. Van Praagh rejoined Battalion from Base details, and was attached to Brigade Hd Qrs 188th Inf. Bde. Lieutenant Lewa rejoined the Battalion from leave.	S/H
—.—			41 O.R. moved to ROBECQ	

WAR DIARY

Place	Date	Hour	Summary of Events and Information	Remarks
ANGRES II.	8th April.		5 Privates wounded.	
— " —	9th April.		Ch/1020 S Pte. T. Grayson killed, 4. O.R. wounded. Captain V. H. S. Jones and Captain Goldsmith joined battalion. Lieutenant McB WOOD and 22 other ranks joined.	J.H. J.H.
— " —	10th April.		Captain Jones and Goldsmith reported to Hd. Qrs in MECHANICS. Captain Jones appointed to command "D" Company, and Capt. Goldsmith to command C Company. Lieut. Woods posted to A Company.	J.H.
— " —	11th April		4. O.R. wounded. Enemy shelling of communication trenches fairly heavy, a large number of gas shell being fired into vicinity of MECHANICS.	J.H.
— " —	12th April		Ch. 1675. S. Pte. C. Heath killed, 3 other ranks wounded	J.H.
— " —	~~13th April~~ J.H.		~~2 other ranks wounded~~ Enemy bombarded front line trenches very heavily during the night, causing a large amount of damage to the trenches. Lieutenant C. West to Hospital. Orders received that the ANSON Battalion would relieve the 1st Bn. R.M.L.I. 1 Officer and 1 N.C.O. per Company, advanced party, Anson battalion arrived to take over the line. Lieutenant Mc B. Wood sent back to LABOURSE with orders to return to England next day	
	13th April		2 Privates wounded. Orders received that the 1st Bn. R.M.L.I. would be relieved by the 3rd Bn Rifle Brigade. Officers of this battalion reported at Hd. Qrs 1.45 pm and moved into the line. The Officers of ANSON Battalion being withdrawn. Relief to commence 8.0 pm	J.H.

Army Form C. 2118

WAR DIARY

Place	Date	Hour	Summary of Events and Information	Remarks
~~LA BOURSE~~ ANGRES II Sector	1917 13th April.		At 3.15 pm. orders were received to send out a Battle Patrol into Enemy trenches near BULLY Craters, to ascertain if he had vacated them. At 4.0 pm orders were received that 3 Patrols had to move out, on the right, centre, and left. The right Patrol moved up the enemy communication trenches to ANGRES, entering the Quarry on the Northern edge of this town, - large dugouts had been made in this Quarry. The Patrol then searched the BOIS de ROLLENCOURT, and entered ROLLENCOURT village. The right Patrol was commanded by 2nd Lt J. KENNY The left Patrol under 2nd Lieut. F. S. MARSH left our front line at PICK AXE Corner, and entered German trench immediately opposite; moved along the communicating trenches to the CITE DES CORNAILLES, & to the Southern edge of LIEVIN, returning via. RED MILL. All these places were found clear of the enemy.	Ref. Map:- 1/1. Trench Map LENS. 36c SW1. 1/10000

A.F.C. 2118

WAR DIARY

Place	Date	Hour	Summary of Events and information	Remarks
ANGRES II Sector	13.4.17		At 9.0 pm. Posts had been established at M 21 C 25.85 (left Post), M 21 C 60 15 (right post), M 21 C 10.00 (Support Post). ~~At 9.30 pm~~ the German 1st line forming the Reserve line. At 9.30 pm the relief by 3rd Rifle Brigade commenced, and was completed at 2.45 am. Casualties 2. O.R. wounded.	JH Ref. Map Trench Map LENS 36 C.S.W. 1 Edition 8.A 1/10000
	14.4.17		Companies marched back to billets as follows:- H.Q. and D Company to BULLY GRENAY, A Company to LES BREBIS, B and C Companies to FOSSE X. Battalion vacated billets at 2.30 pm and marched to BOUVIGNY-BOYEFFLES. Ch 1475 Pte C. HEATH buried BULLY GRENAY Cemetery.	JH
	15.4.17		Battalion vacated billets at BOUVIGNY BOYEFFLES and marched to MAROEUIL.	JH
	16.4.17		Battalion cleaning arms & equipment.	
	17.4.17		Battalion employed cleaning and repairing roads.	JH
	18.4.17		Battalion employed cleaning and repairing roads. Lieut Van Praagh rejoined Battalion from Brigade Hd Qrs. C.O. and 4 Company Officers proceeded to view front line system at BAILLEUIL	JH
	19.4.17		Battalion employed cleaning and repairing roads. Major Ozanne, Capt Huskisson, + 4 Company Officers proceeded to view front line system.	JH
	20.4.17		Battalion employed cleaning and repairing roads.	JH

Instructions regarding War Diaries and Intelligence Summaries are contained in F. S. Regs., Part II. and the Staff Manual respectively. Title pages will be prepared in manuscript.

WAR DIARY
or
INTELLIGENCE SUMMARY.
(Erase heading not required.)

Army Form C. 2118.

Place	Date	Hour	Summary of Events and Information	Remarks and references to Appendices
MAROEUIL	21st		Battn cleaning & repairing roads. Lieut H. B. van PRAAGH assumes duties of Adjutant vice Capt E.J. HUSKISSON to command "B" Coy	H Barnes
	22		Battn vacated billets & moved to trenches - in Brigade Reserve.	
Line	23		Trenches - large carrying party to GAVRELLE 2 ORs wounded 5 killed 2nd Lieut PERRY wounded	
	24		improving reserve trenches. 1 OR wounded	H Barnes
	25.		moved to (Line) - trenches left Sector of GAVRELLE - 2nd Lt LEES wounded 2/Lt THOMAS gassed	
	26		Front line - 2 OR killed 1 missing 8 wounded - C.O attends conference at Brigade HQ - one company moves to take over line of Battn on left	
	27		Front line - Battn have been ordered to attack OPPY - MERICOURT Line - 2 OR killed - 2 wounded - Battn moves to take up Battle positions at 10pm	H Barnes
	28th		Battn attacked on sector left of GAVRELLE, - OPPY Line at 4.25 Am. Gained objectives but were driven out by counter attacks. Following officer casualties. Lieut Col CARTWRIGHT D.S.O. Capt GOLDSMITH, Capt JONES. Capt PEARSON M.C. ~~[illegible]~~ - 2/Lt ATKINSON 2/Lt EVAN, 2/Lt ROBERTS, 2nd Lt KENNY 2/Lt MARSH	H Barnes
	29th		Battn relieved in line	
	30th		" moved to billets in ÉCOIVRES - resting	
	31st			

H Barnes
Major RMLI
Comdg 1/RM L.I.

A5834 Wt. W4973/M687 750,000 8/16 D. D. & L. Ltd. Forms/C.2118/13.

Confidential.

VOLUME XII.

WAR DIARY

of

1st Battalion, Royal Marines Light Infantry

from

1st May, 1917,

to

31st May, 1917.

To the A.G.'s Office,

63rd (R.N.) Division,

3rd Echelon.

N. Ozanne

Lieut.-Colonel, R.M.L.I.,

Commanding 1st Bn., R.M.L.I.

XII/12

Instructions regarding War Diaries and Intelligence Summaries are contained in F. S. Regs., Part II. and the Staff Manual respectively. Title pages will be prepared in manuscript.

WAR DIARY
or
INTELLIGENCE SUMMARY.
(Erase heading not required.)

Army Form C. 2118.

Place	Date	Hour	Summary of Events and Information	Remarks and references to Appendices
[illegible]	1.5		Bn moved from ECOIVRES to FREVILLERS [illegible]	
FREVILLERS	2.5		[illegible] CORNER [illegible] BASE [illegible] [illegible] Lt. MORGAN [illegible] FA	[illegible]
	3.5		Training [illegible] 18 [illegible] BASE	
	4.5			
	5.5			
	6.5			[illegible]
	7.5		[illegible] ECOIVRES	
	8.5		Bn moved by route march [illegible] A 28 [illegible] ECOIVRES [illegible]	
ECOIVRES	9.5		Bn in trenches	[illegible]
[illegible]	10		working on GREEN LINE [illegible]	
	11.5		[illegible] new lines [illegible] 10 OR [illegible] BASE	[illegible]
	12.5		Moved [illegible] A 28 [illegible] GREEN LINE [illegible]	
	13.5		[illegible] BASE GREEN LINE [illegible]	
	14.5		[illegible]	
	15.5		[illegible]	
	16.5		Lieut. [illegible] LIGHTWOOD + 10 OR's joined Bn.	[illegible]
	17.5		Lieut. [illegible] A Coy. Lieut. LIGHTWOOD Transport [illegible]	
	18.5		Bn [illegible] 2 Companies [illegible] X [illegible] X Co. [illegible] Coy	

A5834 Wt. W4973/M687 750,000 8/16 D. D. & L. Ltd. Forms/C.2118/13.

Instructions regarding War Diaries and Intelligence Summaries are contained in F. S. Regs., Part II. and the Staff Manual respectively. Title pages will be prepared in manuscript.

WAR DIARY
or
INTELLIGENCE SUMMARY.
(Erase heading not required.)

Army Form C. 2118.

Place	Date	Hour	Summary of Events and Information	Remarks and references to Appendices
[illegible]	18		CO. [illegible] GALLELLE [illegible] [illegible]	
LINE	19		Batt. [illegible] GALLELLE - No [illegible] CLOSE SUPPORT TRENCHES [illegible] [illegible] GALLELLE [illegible]	(Branei)
	20		[illegible] 3 ORs KILLED & 12 wounded	—
	21		1 killed & 4 wounded. [illegible] WHITEHEAD to UK [illegible] day	(Branei)
	22		No casualties. Quiet day	
	23		2 ORs wounded 1 OR missing — [illegible] BROWN [illegible] slightly wounded. Afterwards [illegible] missing [illegible]	
	24		2 OR killed 4 wounded [illegible]	(Branei)
	25		4 OR wounded. Quiet day with occasional shells.	
	26		1 wounded. Nothing [illegible]	
	27		4 wounded [illegible] GALLWORK [illegible] [illegible] 'X' Co. [illegible] 2/Lt [illegible] to UK leave [illegible] [illegible] WINDMILL MAZE	
	28		~~No casualties~~ 6 wounded — [illegible] otherwise [illegible] [illegible] work on WINDMILL MAZE - CORPS & [illegible] [illegible]	(Branei)
	29		No casualties, very quiet. [illegible] 2nd Lieut. EVANSON [illegible] from BASE	
	30		[illegible] relieved & occupy SUPPORT TRENCHES. No casualties	(Branei)
	31		digging communication trench to SUPPORT LINE [illegible] day - no casualties	—

H. Branei Lieut Col

Confidential.

VOLUME XIII.

War Diary.

1st Battalion Royal Marine Light Infantry.

From

1st June 1917.

To

30th June 1917.

To the A.Gs Office at the Base.

63 rd Division.

3rd Echelon.

[signature]

Lieut Colonel R.M.L.I.

Comdg 1st Battalion. R.M.L.I.

4

Vol 13

63

Instructions regarding War Diaries and Intelligence Summaries are contained in F. S. Regs., Part II. and the Staff Manual respectively. Title pages will be prepared in manuscript.

WAR DIARY
or
INTELLIGENCE SUMMARY.
(*Erase heading not required.*)

Army Form C. 2118.

Place	Date	Hour	Summary of Events and Information	Remarks and references to Appendices
RESERVE TRENCHES	1.6.17		usual trench routine – digging communication trench from REDLINE 2 ORs wounded	
~~[illegible]~~	2.6.17		do – 1 OR wounded do 38 ORs from Base Depôt	[initials]
GAVRELLE	3.6.17		do do 9 ORs buried, effects forwarded to respective Bns	[initials]
	4.6.17		do 2 ORs killed 5 wounded	
	5.6.17		do 1 Company working on FOXEY TRENCH remainder on CT.	[initials]
	6.6.17		do no casualties	
	7.6.17		do do 3 officers from Base Depôt. R.A. [illegible], H. SMITH & J.M. SMITH	[initials]
	8.6.17		do no working party. Officers & OR from relieving Bn up viewing line & taking over.	
	9.6.17		relieved by 18th West Yorks Regt march to ROCLINCOURT, in bivouacs	[initials]
ROCLINCOURT	10.6.17		vacated camp & marched to MARDIEUL in billets. Clean & roomy	[initials]
MARDIEUL	11.6.17		First day devoted to cleaning etc Lieuts WEST & LOWDELL from BASE Depôt	
	12.6.17		Training commenced. Bath parades in training area at 6 am – works till 10 am & rests during hot part of day – then parades again 4.30 pm – 5.30 pm. specialist instruction & firing.	[initials]
	13.6.		Training continued.	[initials]
	14.6		" " morning hours of parade altered to 7 am & continuing to 10.30 am	[initials]
	15.6.		Training continued – 2/Lieut H.A. BASS & 34 ORs from Base	
	16.6.		" "	[initials]
	17.6		Church Parade in morning – no training	[initials]

(A7092). Wt W12839/M1293 75,0.0. 1/17. D. D. & L., Ltd. Forms/C.2118/14.

Instructions regarding War Diaries and Intelligence Summaries are contained in F. S. Regs., Part II. and the Staff Manual respectively. Title pages will be prepared in manuscript.

WAR DIARY

or

INTELLIGENCE SUMMARY.

(Erase heading not required.)

Army Form C. 2118.

Place	Date	Hour	Summary of Events and Information	Remarks and references to Appendices
MARDIEUL	18.6		Routine as previously stated	R.H.P.W.
	19.6			
	20.6		Inspection by Admiral LORD Lo BERESFORD at 2pm – No Coy parades in afternoon	R.H.P.W.
	21.6		Usual routine – Battn preparing to move.	
	22.6		Bn moved to BELLINCOURT (NEAR [illegible]) by [illegible] at 7 am [illegible] bivouacs & dugouts in old GERMAN LINE	R.H.P.W.
	23.6		Work commenced on railway far side of [illegible] – [illegible] Road from 4 – 10 am – 1½ hours specialist instruction in afternoon	R.H.P.W.
	24.6		Working as above – church parade at [illegible] am Major FLETCHER joined Bn from Base	R.H.P.W. R.H.P.W.
	25.6		Work on railway continued – specialist instruction in evening	
	26.6		"	R.H.P.W.
	27.6			
	28.6		Bn moved from BELLINCOURT to BRAY – in billets [illegible] arriving about 7.45 pm – good accommodation – 16 OR from Base	R.H.P.W.
	29.6		Bn [illegible] re-commenced 7am – 10.30 am – specialist instruction in afternoon. 2nd Lieut CARRUTHERS to [illegible] CORPS SCHOOL – [illegible] duty as [illegible]	R.H.P.W.
	30		Same routine – 9 OR from Base Lieut CORNISH proceeded to Eng – 2 months leave as [illegible]	R.H.P.W.

[signature]
Lieut Col R.M.L.I.
Comdg [illegible]

(A7092). Wt W12839/M1293 750,000. 1/17. D. D. & L., Ltd. Forms/C.2118/14.

CONFIDENTIAL.

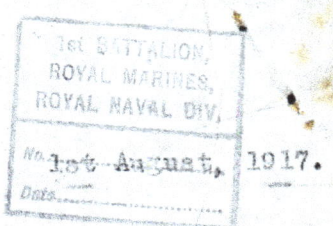

1st August, 1917.

War Diary

of

1st Battalion, Royal Marines Light Infantry,

from

1st July, 1917,

to

31st July, 1917.

To the A.G.'s Office,

3rd Echelon.

E K Fletcher

Major, R.M.L.I.,

Commanding 1st Battalion, R.M.L.I.

Instructions regarding War Diaries and Intelligence Summaries are contained in F. S. Regs., Part II, and the Staff Manual respectively. Title pages will be prepared in manuscript.

WAR DIARY
or
INTELLIGENCE SUMMARY.
(Erase heading not required.)

Army Form C. 2118.

Place	Date	Hour	Summary of Events and Information	Remarks and references to Appendices
BRAY	1st July		Battalion training carried on during past two days suspended to-day. Battalion attended Divine Service in recreation hut near BRAY; service conducted by Chaplain to 2nd R.M.L.I. Lieut.-Colonel H. Ozanne, D.S.O., Commanding 1st R.M.L.I. attended conference at 188th Infantry Brigade Headquarters.	JOms.
BRAY	2nd July		Battalion training from 8 A.M. to 10 A.M. Battalion moved from BRAY to ROCLINCOURT, leaving BRAY at 1.30 P.M., marching via MAROEUIL and overland track thence to ROCLINCOURT and arriving at ROCLINCOURT at 5 P.M. Battalion in huts in WAKEFIELD CAMP in B.28.C. W. of ROCLINCOURT.	JOms. Ref. Sheet 51B N.W.
ROCLINCOURT	3rd July		Battalion moved from WAKEFIELD CAMP this evening and relieved 11th Batt. E. Yorks in the line - ~~left~~ right (JOms) sub sector (GAVRELLE). Relief was quiet, but difficult on account of bad condition of trenches. Battalion occupied front line from right of WINDMILL at C.19.C.7.3 to junction of CAIRO ALLEY and CADORNA TRENCH at C.19.C.4.9. Front line held by three companies with one company in immediate support. Battalion Headquarters in MARINE TRENCH.	JOms. Ref. Map. IZEL-HOF 6.7.17.
IN THE LINE	4th July.		Normal trench routine carried out during the day, and usual carrying-parties by night. This evening battalion front was extended southwards to junction of THAMES ALLEY and CHICO TRENCH at C.25.a.5.8.	JOms. Ref. Map. IZEL-HOF 6.7.17.
— " —	5th July		This morning, company holding left of battalion front made preparations for rushing and capturing enemy strong-point in CRUMPET TRENCH at C.19.d.00.75, but attempt had to be abandoned on account of enemy activity. During day organised sniping with good results was carried out on above strong-point, where was continual hostile movement. Casualties:- 1.O.R. killed + 1 O.R. wounded. 1 O.R. accidentally killed in front-line trench.	JOms. Ref. Map. IZEL-HOF. 6.7.17.

(A7092). Wt. W12539/M1293. 750,000. 1/17. D. D. & L., Ltd. Forms/C.2118/14.

Instructions regarding War Diaries and Intelligence Summaries are contained in F. S. Regs., Part II. and the Staff Manual respectively. Title pages will be prepared in manuscript.

WAR DIARY
or
INTELLIGENCE SUMMARY.
(Erase heading not required.)

Army Form C. 2118.

Place	Date	Hour	Summary of Events and Information	Remarks and references to Appendices
IN THE LINE	1917 6th July		Major-General Lawrie, C.B., D.S.O., ~~[illegible]~~ (Jons) G.O.C. 63rd (R.N) Division made a tour of the battalion front to-day. Normal trench routine observed.	Jons.
— " —	7th July		This morning 4 O.R. wounded and 1 O.R. killed, by enemy trench-mortar fire on company holding centre of battalion front. This evening battalion was relieved by 2nd R.M.L.I. and moved into support in NAVAL and MARINE TRENCHES, with BATT. Headquarters in NAVAL TRENCH. Relief was quiet, but weather rainy.	Jons.
— " —	8th July		Part of day spent by battalion in draining and clearing up mud caused by previous night's rain, and in improving shelters in NAVAL and MARINE TRENCHES.	Jons.
— " —	9th July		At 3 A.M. 6 O.R. were wounded ~~together~~. Battalion working on ~~trenches~~ occupied from 8 A.M. to 12.30 P.M. Major-General Lawrie, C.B., D.S.O., G.O.C. 63rd (R.N) Division and Brigadier-General Hutchinson, C.M.G., D.S.O., G.O.C. 188th Infantry Brigade, made a tour of the battalion's lines to-day.	Jons.
— " —	10th July		Battalion continued work as for previous two days on NAVAL and MARINE TRENCHES. 52 re-inforcements from 63rd (R.N). Infantry Base Depot. 1 N.C.O. to Lewis Gun course at LE TOUQUET. 2 O.R. to Signal course at ORVILLE.	Jons.
— " —	11th July		During forenoon improvement and cleaning of support line as on previous day. To-night battalion relieved 2nd R.M.L.I. in right sub-sector (GAVRELLE); relief was easy and quiet. Battalion extended in front line from a point in CHICO TRENCH at C.25.a.5.8 on the right to junction of CAIRO ALLEY and CADORNA TRENCH at C.19.c.4.9. The front line held by ~~three~~ companies - "D", "B" and "C" Companies from right to left - with one company in immediate support and Battalion Headquarters in MARINE TRENCH. 1 O.R. in "C" Company accidentally wounded.	Jons. Ref. map 51B.N.W. 1/20,000 (?) 6.7.17.

(A7092) Wt W12839/M1293 75,000 1/17. D. D. & L., Ltd. Forms/C.2118/14.

Instructions regarding War Diaries and Intelligence Summaries are contained in F. S. Regs., Part II. and the Staff Manual respectively. Title pages will be prepared in manuscript.

WAR DIARY
or
INTELLIGENCE SUMMARY.
(Erase heading not required.)

Army Form C. 2118.

Place	Date	Hour	Summary of Events and Information	Remarks and references to Appendices
IN THE LINE	12th July.		Normal trench routine observed during day. To-night digging was commenced to connect the extreme right of WINDMILL TRENCH with left of CHICO by a trench running in front of the WINDMILL. Casualties: 1 O.R. wounded. Lieut. Lowdell rejoined battalion from hospital.	JSMS. Ref. Map 12EL-HDF 6.7.17.
— " —	13th July		Major-General Lawrie, C.B., D.S.O., G.O.C. 63rd (R.N.) Division, and Brigadier-General Hutchinson, C.M.G., D.S.O., G.O.C. 188th Infantry Brigade made a tour of battalion's lines to-day. Lieut.-Colonel H. Ozanne, D.S.O., to hospital; Major E.K. Fletcher to command battalion. Casualties – 1 Sergeant and 1 O.R. killed; 1 O.R. wounded.	JSMS
— " —	14th July		2/Lieut. B.G. Evanson proceeded to 1st Army School. 2/Lieut. Edwards and Lieut. S.S. Easterbrook to PERNES – former to Corps Lewis Gun School, latter to Corps Infantry Course. 7 O.R. reinforcements from 63rd (R.N.) Infantry Base Depôt. 2 N.C.O.s to Corps Infantry Course at PERNES. 2 O.R. to Corps Bombing School; 2 O.R. to Corps Lewis Gun School – both at PERNES. Battalion relieved in the line by 2nd R.M.L.I.; relief was difficult on account of bad weather and enemy retaliation after raid on his trenches S.E. of GAVRELLE. Casualties – 2 O.R. killed and 1 O.R. wounded. Battalion to support line.	JSMS. JSMS
— " —	15th July		2/Lieut. R.M. Snider and 17 O.R. reinforcements joined battalion to-day from 63rd (R.N.) Infantry Base Depôt. Considerable part of day spent by battalion in NAVAL and MARINE TRENCHES in clearing up blocks caused by enemy shell-fire on previous evening and in repairing shelters blown in. Casualties: 2 O.R. wounded.	JSMS.

(A7092). Wt W12839/M1293 750,000. 1/17. D. D. & L., Ltd. Forms/C.2118/14.

Instructions regarding War Diaries and Intelligence Summaries are contained in F. S. Regs., Part II. and the Staff Manual respectively. Title pages will be prepared in manuscript.

WAR DIARY
or
INTELLIGENCE SUMMARY.
(Erase heading not required.)

Army Form C. 2118.

Place	Date	Hour	Summary of Events and Information	Remarks and references to Appendices
IN THE LINE	16th July.		Battalion engaged working in support as on previous day. Casualties: 1 O.R. wounded.	JDMS
—"—	17th July.		Battalion relieved 2nd R.M.L.I. in line this evening, and was relieved in support by ~~the~~ Anson Battalion, R.N.D., the 2nd R.M.L.I. going into reserve at MAISON BLANCHE. The relief was lengthy but quiet. Battalion front extended from a point in CHICO TRENCH at C.25.a.5.8 northwards to junction of CAIRO ALLEY and CADORNA TRENCH at C.19.c.4.9., the line being held by "D", "A" and "C" Companies from right to left, with one company in immediate support and battalion headquarters in MARINE TRENCH. Major E. J. Huskisson, M.C., from "B" Company to Battalion Headquarters as 2nd in Command; 2/Lieut. J. W. Thomas, D.C.M., M.M., to command "B" Company temporarily.	Ref. Map ZZEL-HOF 6-7-17.
—"—	18th July.		2/Lieut. Jones to Lewis Gun Course at G.H.Q. School at LE TOQUET. Lieut. Lowdell to ROCLINCOURT. Major Huskisson, M.C. from Battalion Headquarters to command "A" Company vice Captain J. T. GALLIFORD to ROCLINCOURT. During night work was begun on a new trench running in front of the WINDMILL from a point in CECIL TRENCH N.E. of the WINDMILL to Northern end of CHICO. Enemy activity marked on this front and fire very heavy.	JDMS
—"—	19th July		Reinforcements (8 O.R.) from XIII Corps Draft Training Depot joined battalion to-day. One light Draught Horse which had its back broken had to be shot this morning. Normal trench routine observed during the day; usual working and carrying parties by night. Heavy enemy barrage on CHICO TRENCH and CHICO SUPPORT from 11.10 A.M. to 12.30 P.M. 4 O.R. wounded (1 afterwards returning to duty) during this barrage.	JDMS

Instructions regarding War Diaries and Intelligence Summaries are contained in F. S. Regs., Part II. and the Staff Manual respectively. Title pages will be prepared in manuscript.

WAR DIARY
or
INTELLIGENCE SUMMARY.
(Erase heading not required.)

Army Form C. 2118.

Place	Date	Hour	Summary of Events and Information	Remarks and references to Appendices
IN THE LINE	20th July		Captain J. T. Galliford from ROCLINCOURT to command "A" Company; Major Huskisson, M.C., to Battalion Headquarters as 2nd in Command. At 3 A.M. this morning the HOWE battalion on our right made a successful raid on the enemy trenches, and enemy opened a very heavy barrage on our support and communication trenches, inflicting several casualties. Total casualties reported for day – 5. O.R. killed, 1 Sergeant and 15. O.R. wounded (one afterwards died of wounds and 2 were returned to duty). 2/Lieut. R. F. Orfeur joined battalion to-day from 63rd (R.N) Infantry Base Depôt.	J.S.M.S.
— " —	21st July		Lieut. Lowdell rejoined battalion from ROCLINCOURT. Casualties – 2. O.R. wounded. This morning new trench traced out on 18-7-17 was dug all the way through to an average depth of 2'6". Major-General Lawrie, C.B., D.S.O., G.O.C. 63rd (R.N) Division, visited Battalion Headquarters to-day and expressed great satisfaction at the work done by the battalion in digging new front-line mentioned above.	J.S.M.S.
— " —	22nd July.		9. O.R. joined [redacted] battalion from 63rd (R.N) Infantry Base Depôt. Lieut. Lowdell to Hospital. Casualties :- 1. O.R. wounded. Enemy aeroplane was brought down after aerial fight on our front; machine fell burning and crashed to earth.	J.S.M.S.
— " —	23rd July.		Normal trench routine carried out. On night 23/24-7-17. battalion was relieved by 2nd R.M.L.I., and proceeded to reserve at MAISON BLANCHE.	J.S.M.S.
MAISON BLANCHE	24th July.		Battalion accommodated at MAISON BLANCHE in tents, bivouacs and dug-outs. Day spent in general cleaning-up and company re-organisation. Lieut.-Colonel H. Ozanne, D.S.O., rejoined battalion from hospital.	J.S.M.S.

A5834 Wt. W4973/M687 750,000 8/16 D. D. & L. Ltd. Forms/C.2118/13.

Instructions regarding War Diaries and Intelligence Summaries are contained in F. S. Regs., Part II. and the Staff Manual respectively. Title pages will be prepared in manuscript.

WAR DIARY
or
INTELLIGENCE SUMMARY.
(Erase heading not required.)

Army Form C. 2118.

Place	Date	Hour	Summary of Events and Information	Remarks and references to Appendices
MAISON BLANCHE	25th July.		Major E. J. Huskisson, M.C., to command "B" Company. Lieuts. K. E. Champness and D. A. Pipe, and 2/Lieuts. E. C. Bennett, P. G. Cracknell, C. L. C. McKeand, C. E. Mennell, B. C. Pipfett and W. C. Williamson, rejoined battalion to-day from 67th (R.N.) Infantry Base Depôt. Platoons to one hour's parade under platoon commanders at 9 A.M.; specialist instruction from 11 A.M. to 12 noon.	JBM3.
— " —	26th July		Routine as for 25.7.17. 2/Lieut. Jones rejoined battalion from Lewis Gun Course at G.H.Q. School at Le Touquet. 150 men and 5 officers detailed this evening to carry gas cylinders to near GAVRELLE. No casualties during operation.	JBM3.
— " —	27th July		Routine as for 26.7.17.	JBM3.
— " —	28th July		Routine as for 27.7.17. Lieut.-Colonel H. Ozanne, D.S.O., and Captain & Quartermaster T. H. Burton to leave. Major E. J. Huskisson to Battalion Headquarters as 2nd in command; Lieut. D. A. Pipe to command "B" Company. 1 officer and 60 O.R. detailed to work on Red Line to-night.	JBM3.
— " —	29th July		Church Parade at 11.0 A.M. cancelled owing to heavy rain. Captain J. T. Galliford and 2/Lieut. P. G. Cracknell to leave to-day. 9 O.R. reinforcements joined battalion from XIII Corps Draft Training Depôt.	JBM3.

A5834 Wt. W4973/M687 750,000 8/16 D. D. & L. Ltd. Forms/C.2118/13.

Instructions regarding War Diaries and Intelligence Summaries are contained in F. S. Regs., Part II. and the Staff Manual respectively. Title pages will be prepared in manuscript.

WAR DIARY
or
INTELLIGENCE SUMMARY.
(Erase heading not required.)

Army Form C. 2118.

Place	Date	Hour	Summary of Events and Information	Remarks and references to Appendices
MAISON BLANCHE	30th July.		Battalion was relieved in reserve by the Nelson Battalion, R.N.D., and proceeded by route march to BEVERLEY CAMP near ROCLINCOURT. Battalion accommodated there in tents. Orders received that battalion, while in BEVERLEY CAMP, will act as reserve battalion for 190th Infantry Brigade holding left sub-sector of the front.	JBMcB.
ROCLINCOURT	31st July.		5 O.R. sent to-day to 1st Army Rest Camp. 5 O.R. sent to XIII Corps School, PERNES, 2 for instruction in Lewis Gun, 2 for instruction in bombs and 1 for instruction in Stokes Trench Mortars. Battalion to training from 8 A.M. to 10.30 A.M. and from 3.0 P.M. to 4.30 P.M.	JBMcB.

C.K. Fletcher
Major
Commanding 1st Batt. R.M.L.I.

CONFIDENTIAL. 1/9/1917.

VOLUME XII.

W A R   D I A R Y

of

1st BATTALION, ROYAL MARINES LIGHT INFANTRY,

from

1st AUGUST, 1917,

to

31st AUGUST, 1917.

Lieut.-Colonel, R.M.L.I.,

Commanding 1st Battalion, R.M.L.I.

To the A.G.'s Office,

63rd (R.N.) Division,

3rd Echelon.

Instructions regarding War Diaries and Intelligence Summaries are contained in F. S. Regs., Part II. and the Staff Manual respectively. Title Pages will be prepared in manuscript.

WAR DIARY
or
INTELLIGENCE SUMMARY
(Erase heading not required.)

Army Form C. 2118

Place	Date	Hour	Summary of Events and Information	Remarks and references to Appendices
Dearnby camp.	1.8.17.		Battn training suspended on a/c of rain. Companies tested in small box respirators at St. Catherine. Lecture at (64 C.I.I.) Divn theatre on musketry attended by 1 off. and n.c.o per coy. Intelligence offr and N.C.O. Battn sports carried out.	JmcBW
	2.8.17		Bad weather interfered with training. 83 O.R's from XIII C.D.T.D. O.C. companies attend lecture by Divn Gas officer. at St Catherine.	JmcBW
	3.8.17.		Heavy rain. 2/LT F.C. How joins from England, posted to B coy. 2/LT Brunet from England to C coy.	JmcBW
	~~4.8.17~~ 4.8.17.		Still bad weather. Certain amount of work done at range. L. Guns and rifles.	JmcBW
	5.8.17.		Special service held at Ronchmourt. 2 officers 2 sergts and 18 O.R's represented 1st R.M. Battn. Major Hutchison represented 63rd (RN) Divn.	JmcBW
	6.8.17.		Battn training carried out from 8 AM – 12.45 PM. Sports during afternoon	JmcBW
	7.8.17.		Lt-Col Ozanne D.S.O and Capt Burton from leave. 1 O.R Sanitation course. 7 O.R's Bombing course Brudham Camp.	JmcBW
	8.8.17.		Battn relieved Hawke Battn RND in line (GAVRELLE) night of 7/8th Insts. Relief quiet. Normal trench routine observed during day. Usual working and carrying parties by night. Pairs of T.M. gas projectiles found in CHORE Trench and sent to Brigade Hqrs. A/Capt Yellford reported sick on leave	JmcBW
	9.8.17.		Weather conditions bad. Battn cleaning and draining trenches. Quiet day occasional shelling. 4 O.R. wounded.	JmcBW
	10.8.17.		T. Capt. H.B. Van Praag to F.A. 1 St Catherine. 2/LT. B. J. Franson from course at Boulogne. Weather improved. Normal trench routine. Situation quiet. 2. wounded and 1 killed.	JmcBW
	11.8.17.		Normal trench routine. Weather very bad during afternoon.	
	12.8.17		Lt Pipe and Corpl Smith to course at 1st Army School. 2/LT G.D.M. Smith to course 1st Army School sniping at LINGHAM. Battn relieved night of 11/12th by 2nd R.M. Battn. 1st R.M. came into support NAVAL & MARINE Trenches	JmcBW

1875 Wt. W593/826 1,000,000 4/15 J.B.C. & A. A.D.S.S./Forms/C. 2118.

Instructions regarding War Diaries and Intelligence Summaries are contained in F. S. Regs., Part II. and the Staff Manual respectively. Title Pages will be prepared in manuscript.

WAR DIARY
or
INTELLIGENCE SUMMARY
(Erase heading not required.)

Army Form C. 2118

Place	Date	Hour	Summary of Events and Information	Remarks and references to Appendices
NAVAL & MARINE TRENCHES FRONT LINE.	13.8.17.		Normal Trench Routine. Weather changeable. Major Fletcher to Artillery conference at Aire. Situation unchanged.	[initials]
	14.8.17.		" " "	[initials]
	15.8.17.		Night 14/15th relieved 2nd R.M. Battn in front line. A coy on North of Windmill. B coy Windmill. C coy South of Windmill (GAVRELLE) D coy in support in MARINE and RAILWAY support trenches. 2/LT Dix from course. 6 O.R's BREEDHAM camp on bombing course. 1 O.R. wounded. Situation normal.	[initials]
	16.8.17.		Normal Trench Routine. Trenches deepened where necessary. Enemy active with pineapples. S. Major Willard killed. C.Q.M.S. Blackstock wounded (afterwards died) A coy. 2/LT R.G. Bracknell granted ix. of leave.	[initials]
	17.8.17.		Situation quiet. Usual front line routine carried out. New C.T. Trench (CONNAUGHT ALLEY) nearly finished.	[initials]
	18.8.17.		do do do do do do do do.	[initials]
(Reserve) RAILWAY CUTTING	19.8.17.		Normal trench routine. Situation unchanged. 2 O.R. from C.D.T.D. 3 N.C.O's to musketry course. 1st Army.	[initials]
	20.8.17.		Battn relieved night 19/20th by 2nd R.M. Battn. Moved to Reserve Railway Cutting. Very quiet relief. 2/LT McBryde and 2 N.C.O's to Signalling Corps Sig School (ORVILLE) 33 O.R. from C.D.T.D	[initials]
	21.8.17.		Battn in Reserve. Baths etc carried out. Inspection of trench stores. Kit inspection etc. Maj. Fletcher rejoins	[initials]
	22.8.17.		" " " Normal routine. Working parties on Red LINE deepening and revetting.	[initials]
	23.8.17.		" " " 21 O.R. from Base.	
	24.8.17.		Moved to BEAVERLEY camp. ROCLINCOURT. Reserve for the 189th Bde.	
	25.8.17.		Normal routine carried out. Companies practise bombs. 6 O.R to BREEDHAM camp. Bombing.	
	26.8.17.		Church parade. Sunday routine. 11 O.R from C.D.T.D.	
	27.8.17.		Battn training carried out as usual. 2/LT Balcome and 8 O.R. from Base. 1 H.D. Horse to Transport from remount.	
	28.8.17.		" " " 12 O.R from C.D.T.D. 2/LT Donnet on a course 1st Army school of Trench Mortars.	
	29.8.17.		Usual routine. Lt-Col Ozanne to Demonstration on intercommunication. 6 O.R to 1st Army rest camp.	
	30.8.17.		25 O.R from C.D.T.D. & 12 from Base. Battn practises bombs.	
	31.8.17.		Normal Routine. Battn to move into front line on night 1/2nd inst.	

[signature] Lt Col. R.N.L.I.

1875 Wt. W593/826 1,000,000 4/15 J.B.C. & A. A.D.S.S./Forms/C. 2118.

CONFIDENTIAL. 2/10/1917.

VOLUME XII.

W A R D I A R Y

of

1st BATTALION, ROYAL MARINES LIGHT INFANTRY,

from

1st SEPTEMBER, 1917,

to

30th SEPTEMBER, 1917.

H. Ozanne

Lieut.-Colonel, R.M.L.I.,

Commanding 1st Battalion, R.M.L.I.

916

To the A.G.'s Office,

63rd (R.N.) Division,

3rd Echelon.

Instructions regarding War Diaries and Intelligence Summaries are contained in F. S. Regs., Part II. and the Staff Manual respectively. Title Pages will be prepared in manuscript.

WAR DIARY
or
INTELLIGENCE SUMMARY
(Erase heading not required.)

Army Form C. 2118

Place	Date	Hour	Summary of Events and Information	Remarks and references to Appendices
BEVERLEY CAMP.	1/9/17		In Reserve – preparing to move into Line	
ROCLINCOURT Line	2/9/17		Holding GAVRELLE SECTOR. 1. O.R. wounded. 20 ORs from Corps Draft Training Depot	J.B. Evans
"	3/9/17		" " " 2 ORs killed – 1 wded. very Quiet.	
"	4/9/17			
"	5/9/17		" " " T/2nd Lieuts THOMAS, J.W. EVANSON + G.W. KENNY – to wear badges of rank of T/Capt. DRO 2895. 3. ORs wounded	J.B. Evans
"	6/9/17		Holding GAVRELLE SECTOR.	
"	7/9/17		" " " 3. ORs wded – 1 Killed – Lt CORNISH from BASE DÊPOT	
"	8/9/17		To RESERVE CAMP. 22 ORs from BASE. 14 ORs wded. 2 killed.	
MAISON BLANCHE	9/9/17		Cleaning equipment etc. Bn in Reserve. Major HUSKISSON MC. to Base. Major E.K. FLETCHER to Hosp. Lieut CORNISH To leave.	J.B. Evans
"	10/9/17		Wire cutting + working parties RED LINE – remainder Bn – Training	
"	11/9/17		" " " " " " " "	
"	12/9/17		Lieut N. LION + 2nd Lieut. FIELDING previously reported MISSING – found + ^bodies of buried by Bn in front of VISCOUNT ST. also 11 ORs	
LINE	13/9/17		Moved to SUPPORT – NAVAL + MARINE TRENCHES. 2nd Lt MCBRYDE to hospital	J.B. Evans
	14/9/17		In Support. Quiet	
	15/9/17		" " 1 OR. wounded	
	16/9/17		" " Lieut ALDRIDGE + 2nd Lieut GILBERT from BASE.	J.B. Evans

1875 Wt. W593/826 1,000,000 4/15 J.B.C. & A. A.D.S.S./Forms/C. 2118.

Instructions regarding War Diaries and Intelligence Summaries are contained in F. S. Regs., Part II. and the Staff Manual respectively. Title Pages will be prepared in manuscript.

WAR DIARY
or
INTELLIGENCE SUMMARY
(Erase heading not required.)

Army Form C. 2118

Place	Date	Hour	Summary of Events and Information	Remarks and references to Appendices
SUPPORT LINE.	17/9/17		Moving from SUPPORT LINE to BEVERLEY CAMP. Surgn MORGAN R.N. to leave. Revd. Whitehead to leave. 2nd Lt. J.D. H. SMITH to CCS. 9 ORs from BASE.	
BEVERLEY CAMP.	18/9/17		In Reserve – working parties 600 strong to FRONT & RED LINE.	
"	19/9/17		" " " NCOs' class. T/Lieut CRACKNELL to England sick	
"	20/9/17		" " "	
"	21/9/17		" " A/Capt R.H.P. WEST. to Tempy Capt. DRO 2994	
"	22/9/17		moved by bus to billets – BAILLEUL aux CORNAILLES – billets fairly good a bit squashed. (inhabitants friendly) – weather good.	
BAILLEUL AUX CORNAILLES	23/9/17		Church Parade –	
	24/9/17		32 ORs from Base – cleaning up etc	
	25/9/17		commenced training 13 ORs from BASE.	
	26/9/17		Training – R.N.D. system of attack etc.	
	27/9/17		* 2nd Lt CARRUTHERS & 102 ORs joined Bn from BASE. Training, attack on "Pill box" etc	
	28/9/17		Training	
	29/9/17		Training Orders have been received that Bde will probably move on 2/10/17	
	30/9/17		Definite orders received that Bn moves on 2/10/17 from XIIIth Corps to XVIIIth Corps. 2/Lieut H. A. CARRUTHERS to U.K. leave. Capt. D'A. BUNYAN to HOSPITAL.	
			* 2nd Lieut. H.A. CARRUTHERS from Instructor XIIIth C.D.T.D.	

H. Orme
Lieut. Col. Comdg 1/Reg...

1875 Wt. W593/826 1,000,000 4/15 J.B.C. & A. A.D.S.S./Forms/C. 2118.

CONFIDENTIAL.

Headquarters,
1st Battalion,
R.M.L.I.

VOLUME XVII.

W AR D I A R Y

of

1st Battalion,

ROYAL MARINES LIGHT INFANTRY,

from

1st October, 1917,

to

31st October, 1917.

To A.G.'s Office,
3rd Echelon.

Lieut.-Colonel, R.M.L.I.,
Commanding 1st Battalion, R.M.L.I.

Instructions regarding War Diaries and Intelligence Summaries are contained in F. S. Regs., Part II. and the Staff Manual respectively. Title Pages will be prepared in manuscript.

WAR DIARY
or
INTELLIGENCE SUMMARY
(Erase heading not required.)

Army Form C. 2118

Place	Date	Hour	Summary of Events and Information	Remarks and references to Appendices
~~Oct~~	1917		Lieutenant D.A. Pipe to command "C" Company.	
BAILLEUL AU CORNAILLES	October 1st			
	2nd Oct		Captain West, Captain Thomas, Captain Evanson, Lieutenant Pipe, and 2nd Lieut How to Special Course at XVIII Corps School at VOLKERINCKHOVE.	
	~~3rd Oct~~		Battalion marched to TINQUES and entrained for POPERINGHE	
	3rd Oct.		Battalion moved by route march to DIRTY BUCKET Camp, POPERINGHE	
	4th Oct		Major E.J. Huskisson rejoined Battalion and assumed duties of 2nd in Command.	
	5th Oct		Battalion moved by bus to LE NOUVEAU MONDE near WORMHOUDT for training. 2nd Lt J.W. Middleton evacuated to Hospital, 2nd Lt M.K. Gilbert appointed Transport Officer	
	6th Oct		Temp 2nd Lieut R.A. McBryde to England (25/9/17) Authority D.A.G. List No 903. 30/9/17 Temp. Lieut G.A. Lowdell; commission terminated to date 12/9/17. Authority A.G. R.M 3977/17. 29.9.17. Battalion training.	
	7th Oct.		2nd Lt Edwards to Lewis Gun Course at LE TOUQUET. Battalion Training.	
	8th Oct		Battalion Training - The Attack.	
	9th Oct.		Battalion Training - The Attack. 2nd Lt F.C. How appointed Battalion Intelligence Officer	
	10th Oct		Battalion Training - The Attack	

1875 Wt. W593/826 1,000,000 4/15 J.B.C. & A. A.D.S.S./Forms/C. 2118.

Instructions regarding War Diaries and Intelligence Summaries are contained in F. S. Regs., Part II. and the Staff Manual respectively. Title Pages will be prepared in manuscript.

WAR DIARY
or
~~INTELLIGENCE SUMMARY~~
(Erase heading not required.)

Army Form C. 2118

Place	Date	Hour	Summary of Events and Information	Remarks and references to Appendices
~~YOUVEAU MOND~~ WORMHOUDT.	11th October		Battalion carried out Attack practice.	SH
"	12th October		Battalion carried out Attack practice	SH
"	13th October		~~Divine Service~~ SH 2nd Lt. H.A. Carruthers returned from United Kingdom leave. Battalion carried out Attack Practice.	SH
"	14th October		Divine Service	SH
"	15th October		Battalion carried out Attack Practice.	SH
"	16th October		Battalion carried out Attack Practice	SH
"	17th October		Battalion carried out Attack Practice. Information received that Temp. Captain D.A. Bunting has been evacuated to England.	SH
"	18th October		Battalion carried out Attack Practice	SH
"	19th October		Battalion carried out Attack Practice.	SH
"	20th October		Battalion carried out Attack Practice	SH
"	21st October		Divine Service. 2nd Lts. Pepper, McKeand, Orfeur, Meynel proceeded up to front line to take over dispositions.	SH
"	22nd October		Battalion carried out Attack operations, in conjunction with 2nd Bn. R.M.L.I. Temp. Capt. R.H.P. West, A/Capt. J.W. Thomas, Lieut. E. Champness, 2nd Lieuts. P. Edwards, H.G. Bennett, H.A. Carruthers, H.A. Bagg + 43 O.R. moved to 1st Corps Reinforcements. Drawing stores and ammunition.	SH
"	23rd October		Battalion entrained on HERZELE - CASSEL Road, and moved to Camp HERZELE. billets on CANAL Bank - 1000 yards North of YPRES - Transport moved to horse lines 1000x yards W. of BRIELEN. Quartermaster Stores moved to MARSH FARM. 2nd Lt. Orfeur wounded.	SH
"	24th October		Battalion drew 2 days rations etc. preparatory to moving into the line. Casualties Killed 1 Private. wounded 4 Ptes. - by bomb from hostile aeroplane	SH

Instructions regarding War Diaries and Intelligence Summaries are contained in F. S. Regs., Part II. and the Staff Manual respectively. Title Pages will be prepared in manuscript.

WAR DIARY
or
INTELLIGENCE SUMMARY
(Erase heading not required.)

Army Form C. 2118

Place	Date	Hour	Summary of Events and Information	Remarks and references to Appendices
CANAL Bank YPRES	24th		Battalion paraded and moved off to take over front line sector from the 11th Royal Scots. Battalion Head Quarters moved to HUBNER FARM. Battalion took over the line INCH HOUSES - BURNS HOUSE - OXFORD HOUSES - line consisted of Shell holes. Dispositions A Company on right, B Company on ~~centre~~ left, C Company in Reserve at WINCHESTER FARM, D Company at WINCHESTER FARM. Following Officers moved up with battalion Lt Col H. Ozanne D.S.O., Capt A.B. Van Roogh, Lt J McB Woods, Surgeon Morgan, 2nd Lt F.C. Hoar. A Company 2nd Lt Stroliman (in command) 2nd Lt H.J. Jones 2nd Lt H Balcomb. B Company A/Captain B.G. Swanson 2nd Lt N.C. Williamson 2nd Lt B.C. Piffet, Act Lieut C.S. Lastebrook. C Company Act Captain D.A. Pope Lieut J.C. Cornish 2nd Lt C.E. Mennell 2nd Lt E.C. Bennet. D Company Lieut J.D. Aldridge (in command) 2nd Lt M. McKeand. ~~Major Huskisson to Bde H.Qrs (Q Branch)~~ - 2nd Lt Snider appointed Bde Dump Officer	AH
In the line	25th Oct		Battalion Head Quarters moved forward to BURNS House. Battalion commenced to line up on the tape at 8.0 pm. 2 platoons of D Company moving up to OXFORD HOUSES. Frontage of Battalion approximately 900 yards. Depth of objective 900 yards. Furthest limit of Battalion objective - V21 c 85.20 through x of BANFF House to V28 c 5.9 to V28 d 1.3. Direction of advance 30° true bearing from assembly tape. General bearing of assembly tape = 310° true bearing.	AH

1875 Wt. W593/826 1,000,000 4/15 J.B.C. & A. A.D.S.S./Forms/C. 2118.

Instructions regarding War Diaries and Intelligence Summaries are contained in F. S. Regs., Part II. and the Staff Manual respectively. Title Pages will be prepared in manuscript.

WAR DIARY
or
INTELLIGENCE SUMMARY
(Erase heading not required.)

Army Form C. 2118

Place	Date	Hour	Summary of Events and Information	Remarks and references to Appendices
In the line	25th October		The intention was for the 188th Inf Bde to attack, the ANSON Bn and the 1st R.M.L.I attacking the 1st Objective, the HOWE Bn and the 2nd Bn RMLI ~~moving~~ passing through to the 2nd Objective. The total Divisional frontage occupied by the battalion in front line was 1500 yards. The Boundaries of 1st Objective 1st Bn R.M.L.I were – on right from S of INCH HOUSES to V.28 a 2.3 on left LEKKERBOTERBEEK Stream at V.26 b.0.6 thence line of stream to V.21 c.5.1 through E of MORAY HOUSE to V.21 d.8.8. 2nd Lt F.C. HOW returned from HUBNER Farm to Bde Hd Qrs (Q Branch) CANAL Bank. Strength of Battalion in the line, to carry out the attack, 16 Officers and 597 other ranks. Revd W Whitehead at Dressing Station.	AH
— " —	26th Oct		Barrage opened at 5.40 am. Battalion advanced to the Attack under very great difficulties, rain having fallen heavily in the night, shell holes being full of water, & the mud made the ground almost impassable. All objectives were taken including BERKS HOUSES, BANFF HOUSE and BRAY FARM, and the further limit of the objective reached. Considerable casualties were caused during the day by snipers MG fire from the left, where the Bde was unable to advance.	AH
— " —	27th Oct		Battalion holding objective. At about 5.0 pm relief of Battalion by the HAWKE Battalion commenced, the Battalion returning to IRISH FARM. Casualties during the attack & consolidation of position won – Killed Temp Capt D A Pipe, Lt D J Aldridge, 2nd Lt H Balcombe. Died of Wounds 2nd Lt E C Bonnett. Wounded Surgeon P G Morgan R.N. Lt J McBerney Woods (remained at Duty) 2nd Lt E L Scotman, Temp Capt B G Evenson, 2nd Lt W C Wilkinson, 2nd Lt C L C McKi[illegible]	AH

1875 Wt. W593/826 1,000,000 4/15 J.B.C. & A. A.D.S.S./Forms/C. 2118.

Instructions regarding War Diaries and Intelligence Summaries are contained in F. S. Regs., Part II. and the Staff Manual respectively. Title Pages will be prepared in manuscript.

WAR DIARY
or
INTELLIGENCE SUMMARY

(Erase heading not required.)

Army Form C. 2118

Place	Date	Hour	Summary of Events and Information	Remarks and references to Appendices
IRISH FARM	27th Oct	~~7.45 am~~	~~Battalion~~ Casualties amongst Rank + File on the 26th and 27th - 270.	JH
"	28th Oct	9.45 am	Battalion marched to DAMBRE Camp	JH
"	29th		Battalion re organising. drawing Stores and equipment.	JH
"	30th		Battalion training and reorganising. Actg. Lieut. S.S. Easterbrook and 2nd Lt J.R Jones proceeded into the line to take over dispositions with view to a relief. 2nd Lt J McBirney Woods to U.K. Leave.	JH
"	31st		Battalion training and reorganising.	JH

H. [illegible]
Lieut. Col. R.I.R.
Comdg. 9/R.I.R.

1875 Wt. W593/826 1,000,000 4/15 J.B.C. & A. A.D.S.S./Forms/C. 2118.

1st BATTALION R.M.L.I.

WAR DIARY.

From.

1st NOVEMBER 1917.

To.

30th NOVEMBER 1917.

C.G. Farquharson

Major, R.M.L.I.
Commanding 1st Battalion R.M.L.I.

8/128

Instructions regarding War Diaries and Intelligence Summaries are contained in F. S. Regs., Part II. and the Staff Manual respectively. Title Pages will be prepared in manuscript.

WAR DIARY

or

~~INTELLIGENCE SUMMARY~~

(Erase heading not required.)

Army Form C. 2118

VOL. NO 18.

Place	Date	Hour	Summary of Events and Information	Remarks and references to Appendices
DAMBRE CAMP.	1/11/17		Resting & cleaning up	
	2.11.17		" "	
"	3.11.17		" "	
"	4.11.17		" Lt.Col H. Ozanne Dep. to Hospital – Major Huskisson to command	
"	5.11.17		Inspection by Divl General. Batt'n moves to CANAL BANK – Y company attached to OC. 2nd Bn RMLI. for duty in line	W.Ward
CANAL BANK (YSER)	6.11.17		9 ORs Killed 21 wounded 4 missing	
	7.11.17		"Y" Coy from Line. Bn moves to School Camp POPERINGHE AREA by train. Lt.Col. W.T. BROMFIELD – Leicestershire Regt. assumed command of Batt'n.	W.Ward
"	8.11.17		2nd Lt. McKeand to U.K. Leave	
SCHOOL CAMP.	9.11.17		Resting & cleaning up	
"	10.11		Resting & cleaning up. T/Capt THOMAS rejoined Bn from depot Bn. Concert in evening	W.Ward
"	11		Church Parade – Memorial Service for those who fell on Oct. 26th	
"			2nd Lt HENNEL to U.K. leave	W.Ward
"	12.		Bn. vacated SCHOOL CAMP & ~~left~~ moved by route march to Camp at WINNEZEELE (J.11.a. 9.5 Sheet 27)	
WINNEZEELE			Details left out of action – under T/Capt WEST rejoined Batt'n from Depot Batt'n	W.Ward
"	13th		Bn moved by route march to LEDRINGHEM (I2. central Sheet 27)	
LEDRINGHEM	14		T/2nd Lieuts THIRKELL, McADAM, BAZIRE & TAYLOR joined the Batt'n. Armourer Sergt commenced inspection & overhauling of arms.	W.Ward

1875 Wt. W593/826 1,000,000 4/15 J.B.C. & A. A.D.S.S./Forms/C. 2118.

Instructions regarding War Diaries and Intelligence Summaries are contained in F. S. Regs., Part II. and the Staff Manual respectively. Title Pages will be prepared in manuscript.

WAR DIARY
or
~~INTELLIGENCE SUMMARY~~
(Erase heading not required.)

Army Form C. 2118

volume 18.

Place	Date	Hour	Summary of Events and Information	Remarks and references to Appendices
LEDRINGHEM	15.		Billets fairly good. 'D' Coy exchange to larger farm – Kit Inspection etc	
"	16		Refitting – Bathing etc – C.O.'s Conference	
	17		2nd/Lt P. EDWARDS appointed Assistant Adjutant (temporarily) The Band of the RMA played in afternoon.	J Evans
	18.		Divine Service	
	19		Route March – Gas respirator drill in afternoon – Major C.G. FARQUHARSON – RMLI assumed command of Bn – Lt Col. BROMFIELD Leicestershire Regt to H.Q. 42nd Div. Ch. 19621 Pte T. LYSON – Ch. 457/S Pte F. W. MORRIS, Ch 489/S Pte J. H. NASH – awarded the Military Medal for services in action 26.10.17. Lt EASTERBROOK to F.A. – sick	J Evans
	20	AM	Physical Training, Close order ~~+ Bayonet Fighting~~	
		PM.	recreational training	
	21.		do Ch. 16,227 A/Sgt E PRIESTLEY awarded the D.C.M. Inspection by Capt BACKHOUSE C.B. R.N. 50 ORs from BASE 2nd/Lt SNIDER to F.A.	J Evans
	22		Bn moved by Bus to GARDEN CITY CAMP – BRIELEN	J Evans
BRIELEN	23		T/Lt E. WARDEN, G. J. WHARF, & 2/Lts W. J. COOK & G. STUART from BASE	
	24		Working parties on roads at TRIANGLE – specialists remaining behind for instruction	J Evans

1875 Wt. W593/826 1,000,000 4/15 J.B.C. & A. A.D.S.S./Forms/C. 2118.

Instructions regarding War Diaries and Intelligence Summaries are contained in F. S. Regs., Part II. and the Staff Manual respectively. Title Pages will be prepared in manuscript.

WAR DIARY

or

~~INTELLIGENCE SUMMARY~~

(Erase heading not required.)

Volume No 18.

Army Form C. 2118

Place	Date	Hour	Summary of Events and Information	Remarks and references to Appendices
BRIELEN	25.		2nd Lt DIPPET entitled to badges of rank of Captain (Acting) 16/11/ 2nd Lt CARRUTHERS to command "C" Coy – working parties on roads – specialists to instruction	
	26		working parties on roads – specialists to instruction	
	27		" " " " " "	
	28		" " " " " " Lt WHARF to Asst Adj. } Lt HOTHAM to Lg Officer } temporarily	
	29		" " " " " 1 OR killed – 2nd Lt MENNEL from leave	
	30		" " " " 2nd Lt J.R. JONES to F.A.	

C G Fergusson
Major RMLI
Commdg 1st Bn
Royal Marine Light Infantry

1875 Wt. W593/826 1,000,000 4/15 J.B.C. & A. A.D.S.S./Forms/C. 2118.

A/603
2/1/18.

Confidential.

WAR DIARY.

Volume No XV.

1/Battalion, Royal Marines Light Infantry.

From 1/12/17

To 31/12/17.

To, - The A.Gs Office,
At the BASE.

C.G. Farquharson

Lieut Colonel R.M.L.I.

Comdg 1st Battalion, R.M.L.I.

96/19

Instructions regarding War Diaries and Intelligence Summaries are contained in F. S. Regs., Part II. and the Staff Manual respectively. Title pages will be prepared in manuscript.

WAR DIARY
or
INTELLIGENCE SUMMARY.
(Erase heading not required.)

Army Form C. 2118.

1st [illegible]

Place	Date	Hour	Summary of Events and Information	Remarks and references to Appendices
Garden City Camp, near Brielen.	1/12/17 to 5/12/17		Working Parties on "Triangle.	[initials]
			do do	[initials]
Schools Camp near Poperinghe.	6/12/17		Move by route march to Schools Camp.	[initials]
	7/12/17 to 8/12/17		Working Parties and Training.	[initials]
			do do	[initials]
Proven	9/12/17		Move by Route March to PESELHOCK, and entrain for ACHEUX-LE-GRAND.	[initials]
Beaulen court	10/12/17		Detrain ACHEUX-LE-GRAND and move by Route march to 'B' Camp M area BEAULIN COURT.	[initials]
	11/12/17 to 13/12/17		Training	[initials]
			do	[initials]
Rocquigny	14/12/17		Move by Route march to ROCQUIGNY.	[initials]
Etricourt	15/12/17		do do ETRICOURT.	[initials]
			Following Officers joined battalion:– T/Lieut. W. C. Gwynne. T/2nd Lieuts. F. L. Lowden, C. H. Bailey, C. A. R. Lawrence, W. Jaques, H. L. Sayer, H. J. Irwin, H. Horn, W. J. Chalcroft, R. C. Lewis, S. L. Cailes, R. H. Tregidga, W. H. Hughes	[initials] [illegible]

(A7092). Wt W12839/M1293 75,0,0,0 1/17. D. D. & L., Ltd. Forms/C.2118/14.

Army Form C. 2118.

Instructions regarding War Diaries and Intelligence Summaries are contained in F. S. Regs., Part II. and the Staff Manual respectively. Title pages will be prepared in manuscript.

WAR DIARY
or
INTELLIGENCE SUMMARY.
(Erase heading not required.)

1st R.M.L.I.

Place	Date	Hour	Summary of Events and Information	Remarks and references to Appendices
Lechelles	16/12/17		Move by Route march to LECHELLES.	
	17/12/17		Training.	
	18/12/17		T/Lt/Col H Ozanne DSO rejoined battalion.	
	19/12/17		Training.	
	20/12/17		Celebration of Christmas Day	
	21/12/17		Training. Lt Col Ozanne resumed Command of Battalion, Lt Col B G Farquharson to 2nd R.M.L.I.	
Metz	22/12/17		Move by Route march to METZ.	
	23/12/17		Improving billets and training	
	24/12/17		T/Capt R.H.P. West assumes duties of A/Adj during absence of T/Capt A B van Praagh on leave.	
	25/12/17		Improving billets and Routine.	
	26/12/17		A/Lt Col B G Farquharson assumed command of battalion during absence of T/Lt Col H Ozanne D.S.O. on leave. Move to forward area and relieved 2nd batt R.M.L.I. in front line VILLIERS PLOUICH.	
	27/12/17		Consolidation of Trenches	
	28/12/17		3. OR wounded.	

(A7092). Wt W12839/M1293 75,0.0. 1/17. D. D. & L., Ltd. Forms/C.2118/14.

Army Form C. 2118.

WAR DIARY
or
INTELLIGENCE SUMMARY. 1st R.M.L.I.

(*Erase heading not required.*)

*Instructions regarding War Diaries and Intelligence Summaries are contained in F. S. Regs., Part II. and the Staff Manual respectively. Title pages will be prepared in manuscript.

Place	Date	Hour	Summary of Events and Information	Remarks and references to Appendices
In-the-Line	29/12/17		Consolidation of Trenches.	
	30/12/17		do do T/2nd Lt W Jaques + 6 OR wounded	
	31/12/17		do do 1 OR killed, 4 OR wounded.	
			Relieved by 2nd RMLI and move into support VILLERS PLOUICH.	

C G Farquharson

Lt Col

Commanding 1st Bn

Royal Marines Light Infantry

(A7092). Wt W12839/M1293 75,0:0. 1/17. D. D. & L., Ltd. Forms/C.2118/14.

CONFIDENTIAL. 1/2/1918.

VOLUME XVI. XX

W A R D I A R Y

of

1st BATTALION, ROYAL MARINES LIGHT INFANTRY,

from

1st January, 1918,

to

31st January, 1918.

E K Fletcher

Major, R.M.L.I.,

Commanding 1st Battalion, R.M.L.I.

Vol 20

To the A.G.'s Office,

63rd (R.N.) Division,

3rd Echelon.

Instructions regarding War Diaries and Intelligence Summaries are contained in F. S. Regs., Part II. and the Staff Manual respectively. Title pages will be prepared in manuscript.

WAR DIARY
or
INTELLIGENCE SUMMARY.
(Erase heading not required.)

Army Form C. 2118.

1st Bn R.M.L.I.

Place	Date	Hour	Summary of Events and Information	Remarks and references to Appendices
VILLERS PLOUICH	1/1/18		In the support. Supplying working parties for consolidation of line.	
			T/2nd Lieut M. Taylor to F.A.	
			T/Capt B. C. Pyffett to U K leave.	
			1 - OR wounded	
	2/1/18		do Supplying working parties.	
	3/1/18		Working parties as for 1/1/18.	
			T/2nd Lieut Bailey to 2/R.M.L.I. to be attached.	
			" " Cook " "	
			Operation Order No 73	
	4/1/18		A/605 T/Lt Cornish and 1 NCO to 3rd Army Musketry School.	
			A/604 1 OR to 3rd Army Signal School.	
			A/606 6 ORs to V Corps School (LG 12 days)	
			" 4 ORs do (Bombing 12 ")	
			A/608 T/2 Lieut McAdam to V Corps Signal School and 1 OR (6 weeks)	
			Relieved ANSON Bn in Left Sub Sector. (WELSH SUPPORT)	
			T/Capt T.H. Burton from U K leave.	

(A7092). Wt. W12839/M1293. 75,0.0. 1/17. D. D. & L., Ltd. Forms/C.2118/14.

Instructions regarding War Diaries and Intelligence Summaries are contained in F. S. Regs., Part II. and the Staff Manual respectively. Title pages will be prepared in manuscript.

WAR DIARY
or
INTELLIGENCE SUMMARY.
(Erase heading not required.)

Army Form C. 2118.

1st Bn R Ir L I

Place	Date	Hour	Summary of Events and Information	Remarks and references to Appendices
In-the-Line	5/1/18		Capt R. A. Poland from base.	JJ
			" R. H. Campbell "	JJ
			T/2nd Lieut Bailey missing	JJ
			" " (Correction – Killed).	JJ
			28 OR from D W Wing.	JJ
	6/1/18		QM to course of Practical Sanitation.	JJ
			Ytres RTO 1-PM. 92 Rue-de-doullens. Arras.	JJ
			Div letter 1330/9/A 1-1-18.	JJ
			T/2 Lieut Tregidga to Div Wing and 10 OR for Signals to Div Wing.	JJ
			T/2 Lieut Coiles to Brigade Tunnelling Section.	JJ
			Ptes Chemming & Ptes Pike missing from trenches.	JJ
	7/1/18		Operation Order No 74.	JJ
			2 OR wounded.	JJ
	8/1/18		Relieved by 2/RMLI and moved into reserve at METZ.	JJ
			Major C. G. Farquharson to 2/RMLI.	JJ
			" G. K. Fletcher from Brigade.	JJ
			3 OR wounded and 1 killed.	JJ

(A7092). Wt W12839/M1293. 75,000. 1/17. D. D. & L., Ltd. Forms/C.2118/14.

Instructions regarding War Diaries and Intelligence Summaries are contained in F. S. Regs., Part II. and the Staff Manual respectively. Title Pages will be prepared in manuscript.

WAR DIARY
or
INTELLIGENCE SUMMARY
(Erase heading not required.)

1st Bn R.I.L.I.

Army Form C. 2118

Place	Date	Hour	Summary of Events and Information	Remarks and references to Appendices
METZ	9/1/18		Major C.K. Fletcher assumes command of battalion.	P.S.
			Cleaning up, baths etc.	P.S.
			T/2nd Lieut R.C. Lewis to F.A.	P.S.
	10/1/18		Routine and baths, cleaning up etc.	P.S.
			7 OR to UK leave.	P.S.
	11/1/18		Rev. W. Whitehead to England for duty afloat.	P.S.
			Operation Order No 75.	P.S.
			DRO. 3506. Following Officers to be T/Capts.-	P.S.
			A/Capt J Kenny, A/Capt H A Carruthers, A/Capt J. W. Thomas all dated 20/12/17.	P.S.
			DRO. 3507 T/Major C.G. Farquharson to Major dated 1/1/18.	P.S.
			T/Capt H. A. Carruthers 2/1/18 to England sick.	P.S.
	12/1/18		Move into line and relieved ANSON Bn in right sub sector. (PRENTICE TR and HOLLY TR)	P.S.
			1 OR wounded at DEAD MAN'S CORNER	P.S.
			2 Light Draught Horses killed.	P.S.
			3 " " wounded.	P.S.
			2 OR wounded + 1 missing.	P.S.
			T/Lieut. J.S. Easterbrook to UK leave.	P.S.
			T/2nd " P. Edwards "	P.S.
			T/Capt J. W. Thomas to FA.	P.S.

1875 Wt. W593/826 1,000,000 4/15 J.B.C. & A. A.D.S.S./Forms/C. 2118.

Instructions regarding War Diaries and Intelligence Summaries are contained in F. S. Regs., Part II. and the Staff Manual respectively. Title Pages will be prepared in manuscript.

WAR DIARY
or
INTELLIGENCE SUMMARY
(Erase heading not required.)

Army Form C. 2118

1st Bn R. M. L. I.

Place	Date	Hour	Summary of Events and Information	Remarks and references to Appendices
In-the-Line.	13/1/18		Consolidation of Trenches. 1 OR wounded.	
	14/1/18		Major C. J. Huskisson to England. - Consolidation of Line. 5 OR to FA.	
	15/1/18.		Consolidation of Line. 1 OR killed. T/2nd Lieut Holloway to FA. Operation Order No 76 published. 10 OR to FA.	
	16/1/18		Relieved by 2/RMLI and proceed to Support VILLERS PLOUICH. Rev G. G. McGregor from base.	
VILLERS PLOUICH	17/1/18		B.M. 2/9. Report of Instructional Staff complete. Operation Order No 77.	
In-the-Line.	18/1/18		Move from support and relieved ANSON Bn in Left sub sector.	
	19/1/18		Internal relief. Body of T/2nd Lt Bailey recovered and interred at 57C. - R.15. C 85. 92. D.R.O 3548 Major C. G. Farquharson to A/Lt Col dated 20/11/17. Capt Peppett from UK leave.	
	20/1/18		Consolidation of trenches.	
	21/1/18		do	

1875 Wt. W593/826 1,000,000 4/15 J.B.C. & A. A.D.S.S./Forms/C. 2118.

Instructions regarding War Diaries and Intelligence Summaries are contained in F. S. Regs., Part II. and the Staff Manual respectively. Title pages will be prepared in manuscript.

WAR DIARY
or
INTELLIGENCE SUMMARY.
(*Erase heading not required.*)

Army Form C. 2118.

1st Bn R.M.L.I.

Place	Date	Hour	Summary of Events and Information	Remarks and references to Appendices
In-the-Line.	22/1/18		Relieved in left sub sector by 2/RMLI, and move into support VILLERS PLOUICH. Operation Order No 79.	
VILLERS PLOUICH	23/1/18		Relieved by 23rd Bn RF and move by Route march to METZ. Operation Order No 80.	
METZ	24/1/18		Move by rail to ROQUIGNY. "A" Camp.	
ROQUIGNY	25/1/18		Inspection of Equipment etc and cleaning up.	
	26/1/18		Lt Col H Ozanne to be struck off strength in accordance with AG/2158/578.(O) 15-1-18, Working parties.	
	27/1/18		Employed on protection of huts from hostile aircraft.	
	28/1/18		Training and refitting.	
	29/1/18		Major Huskisson to be struck off strength. 2/Lt P. Edwards from UK leave. Duty battalion and protection of huts.	
	30/1/18		Training and protection of huts complete.	
	31/1/18		Training and night operations.	

[signature] Capt
for Commanding Officer,
1st Bn R.M.L.I.

1ST
BATTALION
ROYAL MARINES,
ROYAL NAVAL DIVISION.
No. A 829
Date 9/3/18

Volume XVII

War Diary of 1st Battalion Royal Marines Light Infantry.

From 1st February 1918.

To 28th February 1918.

EK Fletcher

A.G.
Base.

Lieut Colonel R.M.L.I.
Comdg 1/Bn R.M.L.I.

WO 21

Army Form C. 2118.

Instructions regarding War Diaries and Intelligence Summaries are contained in F. S. Regs., Part II. and the Staff Manual respectively. Title pages will be prepared in manuscript.

WAR DIARY
or
INTELLIGENCE SUMMARY.
(Erase heading not required.)

Place	Date	Hour	Summary of Events and Information	Remarks and references to Appendices
ROCQUIGNY.	1/2/18.		All ranks engaged in ~~making~~ putting the camp in a state of defense against hostile Aircraft. 2nd Lt P Edwards to course of signals & liaison with R.F.C.	RAHl.
"	2/2/18.		Duty Battalion to Brigade, finding of all camp fatigues & continuation of work protecting huts against hostile aircraft. Court of Enquiry assembling at Bde. H.Qrs. re loss of Gum boots thigh issued to 188th Inf. Bde. All adjutants of Bns. battled. 1 O.R. joined Bn from Div. Wing.	RAHl.
"	3/2/18		~~Divine~~ Bn attended Divine service in the forenoon. Afternoon devoted to Bde. boxing competition 9 entries from the Bn; finals postponed until next day owing to bad light. Following O.Rs proceeded on courses of instruction: 1 Sgt. 3 Ptes.	RHAl.
"	4/2/18.		Duty Bn. to Bde. all training cancelled. 183 O.Rs erecting new NISSEN hut camp for ANSON Bn. remainder of Bn employed in furnishing camp fatigues & guards. Divisional Commander inspected the work & expressed his approval. Semi finals & finals of boxing competition. Welter weight & feather weight were won. 2nd Lt. P. Edwards rejoined unit from course. Lecture to all officers by D.G.O. on cloud gas attacks & gas shells.	R.H.P.L.
"	5/2/18		Testing of Box respirators, all ranks went through the gas chamber, after which Companies carried out training in accordance with programme. Afternoon devoted to games music supplied by HOOD Bn. band. Lt. D. R. Hall & 2nd Lt. F.C. How to U.K. leave. T/Lt W.C. Gwynne from Infantry Course, 3rd Army School 5/2/18.	RAHl.

Instructions regarding War Diaries and Intelligence Summaries are contained in F. S. Regs., Part II. and the Staff Manual respectively. Title pages will be prepared in manuscript.

WAR DIARY
or
INTELLIGENCE SUMMARY.
(Erase heading not required.)

Army Form C. 2118.

Place	Date	Hour	Summary of Events and Information	Remarks and references to Appendices
ROCQUIGNY	6/2/18		Duty Bn to Bde. 2 officers 86 O.R.s detailed for camp duties. B and C Companies firing on the range. 2/Lt/Capt. H. B. van Praagh M.C. to England with instructions report to War Office for duty in England. 2nd Lt Cross to England to report Commandant PLYMOUTH. Lecture to all officers by O.C 15th Squadron R.F.C. at 6 P.M.	RHHW.
"	7/2/18		Bn to carried out training in accordance with time table. P.M. a demonstration was given by 188th Bde. Machine Gun Coy a barrage concentrated on a selected target. Officers were then detailed to stand between the target & the guns firing in order to accustom them to over head M.G. fire. Lt. Cornish to England with instructions report Commandant PLYMOUTH. Lecture to all officers on "Mask Work" by O.C 149th Field Coy R.E.	RHHW.
"	8/2/18		Bn. duty Bn. to Bde. 90 O.R.s on fatigues + guards. Remainder of Bn. carried out training in accordance with training programme. No. 424/S A/Cpl. J. Sherman awarded Croix de Guerre (Belgium). Bde. cross country Run held to select men to represent the Bde in the Divisional Run, 5 O.R.s from the Bn. chosen.	RHHW.
	9/2/18		Bn. training. A lecture was given by the Rev. J. E. Roberts at ROCQUIGNY subject – "Why the War must go on". 5 officers + 4 N.C.O.s detailed to attend. In the afternoon following Bde	RHHW.
	10		Competitions were held. Battle musketry competition for 1 N.C.O + 8 O.R.s. Wiring Competition. Bn placed 2nd in both events. In the evening Divisional boxing competition held at BARASTRE. Middle Weight won ~~by~~ ~~Knight~~ RHW by No 13924. Cpl. P. KENT.	RHHW.

A7092). Wt. W12839/M1293 750,000. 1/17. D. D & L., Ltd. Forms/C2118/14.

Army Form C. 2118.

Instructions regarding War Diaries and Intelligence Summaries are contained in F. S. Regs., Part II. and the Staff Manual respectively. Title pages will be prepared in manuscript.

WAR DIARY
or
INTELLIGENCE SUMMARY.
(Erase heading not required.)

Place	Date	Hour	Summary of Events and Information	Remarks and references to Appendices
ROCQUIGNY	10/2/18		Bn Duty Bn to Bde usual guards + fatigues furnished. Divine service held in Recreation room at 10.30 AM service taken by Rev. MOORE senior chaplain to Division. Official notification received for 250 O.R^s + 3 officers HOWE Bn. to be attached to Bn. P.M. on 11/2/18.	R H P W.
"	11/2/18.		Training by Coys from 8.30 AM – 10.20 AM. At 11.15 AM 222 O.R^s HOWE Bn + 3 Offs reported to be attached. Rev. E.E. Farquharson reported + appointed C of E chaplain to 1st + 2nd Bns. RMLI Divisional Cross country race won by 190th Bde. 188th Bde. second. At 6 P.M a conference was held by the G.O.C on Trench foot. A.D.M.S + A.A. & Q.M.G attended.	RHPW.
"	12/2/18.		Bn. duty Bn to Bde. usual guards + fatigues furnished. Remainder of Bn training in accordance with programme. A night march was carried out in Gas masks ending with the Bn forming up in close column of companies, leading coy on tape line. Operation order received for pending move into the line. Commanding Officer + Capt RH Poland attended a tank demonstration at BRAY.	RHPW.
"	13/2/18.		Training was cancelled owing to bad weather. Lectures were given by the O.C + by O.C. Coys. O.O. No 181 from Bde H.Q^rs received. Bn. O.O. 81 issued (attached).	RHPW.

A7092). Wt. W12839/M1293 750,000. 1/17. D. D & L., Ltd. Forms/C2118/14.

Instructions regarding War Diaries and Intelligence Summaries are contained in F. S. Regs., Part II. and the Staff Manual respectively. Title pages will be prepared in manuscript.

WAR DIARY
or
~~INTELLIGENCE SUMMARY.~~
(Erase heading not required.)

Army Form C. 2118.

Place	Date	Hour	Summary of Events and Information	Remarks and references to Appendices
ROCQUIGNY	14/2/18		Bn moved by march from ROCQUIGNY to EASTWOOD camp HAVRINCOURT WOOD. Left at 2 P.M arrived at destination at 4 30 P.M. Camp was found to consist of 21 NISSEN huts + averaged about 35-40 men per hut.	RAH
"EASTWOOD" Camp in HAVRINCOURT WOOD	15/2/18		Companies practised artillery formations + assembly for trench to trench attack. Major N.S. Clutterbuck joined as 2nd in command. Camp bombed between 9 P.M + 10 P.M by hostile aircraft. One machine landed with a crew of 1 Off. + 3 O.R.s at P.15.c near YTRES-RUYAULCOURT Rd. 2 slightly injured. Machine was forced to land through engine trouble. Before landing a series of red lights were fired as a signal of distress. On this signal German bombing grounds [illegible] showed a light.	RAH
"	16/2/18		Court martial on Ptes CREMMINGS + PIKE. President Major N.S. CLUTTERBUCK. At 11 AM enemy shelled the camp with H.E + shrapnel also at 1 P.M 1 man wounded. 2nd Lt Taylor proceeded on 7 days gas course. 2nd Lt Stuart rejoined Bn from A.P.M. AMIENS. Hostile aircraft again bombed the camp from 6 30 P.M to about 10 30 P.M no casualties	RAH

A7092). Wt. W12839/M1293 750,000. 1/17. D. D & L., Ltd. Forms/C2118/14.

Army Form C. 2118.

WAR DIARY
or
~~INTELLIGENCE SUMMARY.~~

(Erase heading not required.)

Instructions regarding War Diaries and Intelligence Summaries are contained in F. S. Regs., Part II. and the Staff Manual respectively. Title pages will be prepared in manuscript.

Place	Date	Hour	Summary of Events and Information	Remarks and references to Appendices
~~17/2/18~~ EASTWOOD Camp HAVRINCOURT WOOD	17/2/18.		Operation + administrative orders for taking over the line occupied by HOOD Bn. 189th Bde received from 188th Inf. Bde. Bn operation orders issued as attached. News received that Pte CHEMMINGS escaped from guard room of HOWE Bn afterwards he was recovered. Camp again bombed by hostile aircraft during the evening also very slightly shelled.	RAH
ditto	18/2/18.		Bn rested + everything prepared for taking over the line. Bn entrained at EASTWOOD camp + proceeded by light Railway as far as TRESCAULT. Bn then moved by overland track with [illegible] at 200 yds distance + [illegible] behind platoons relief completed at 11.30 P.M.	RAH
COUILLET SECTOR map ref. LA VACQUERIE $\frac{1}{10,000}$	19/2/18		During the day ~~there~~ was very little hostile shelling. During the evening enemies trench mortars shewed increased activity. Situation remained unchanged during whole day + night. 1 man wounded	RAH
do	20/2/18.		Enemies trench mortars very active against our trenches. Operation order for the relief of Bn by ~~3~~ 2nd H.L.I. and OXFORD and BUCKS L.I. received from Bde. Bn operation order no 83 issued at 6 30 P.M. 2 O.R's killed & 1 ~~[illegible]~~ wounded. 21. O.R's Reinforcements and 6 casuals joined Bn.	RAH

A7092). Wt. W12839/M1293 750,000. 1/17. D. D & L., Ltd. Forms/C2118/14.

Instructions regarding War Diaries and Intelligence Summaries are contained in F. S. Regs., Part II. and the Staff Manual respectively. Title pages will be prepared in manuscript.

WAR DIARY
or
~~INTELLIGENCE SUMMARY.~~
(Erase heading not required.)

Army Form C. 2118.

Place	Date	Hour	Summary of Events and Information	Remarks and references to Appendices
COUILLET Ridge	21/2/18		All arrangements made for relief by 2nd H.L.I and 1 Coy of Oxford and Bucks L.I. Guides were instructed in their duties. 2nd Lt HORNE and Lt. HOTHAM left the line at 9.30 AM for Q.M stores prior to proceeding on a course of instruction on 22/2/18. Sub Lt Corr ANSON Bn attached 1st R.M as signal officer left the line to hospital having put his knee out. Relief completed at 9.30 P.M + Bn proceed via track to TRESCAULT & entrained for YTRES occupying billets in PIONEER Camp.	R.H.R.W.
PIONEER Camp LECHELLE	22/2/18		Companies at disposal of O.C companies and day spent in cleaning arms, equipment and clothing. Instructions received for Bn to move to EASTWOOD camp on 23/24th + relieve HOOD Bn. Operation order no. 84 issued. Lt. HOTHAM + 2nd Lt. HORNE proceeded to V Corps school for General Course of instruction. Lt [illegible] returned off course from 3rd Army Musketry school. 2nd Lt. HOWE from U.K. leave.	R.H.R.W.
ditto	23/2/18		Bn proceeded by Route March to EASTWOOD camp falling in at 1.45 PM arriving at 3.15 PM. 2nd Lt. EDWARDES to hospital sick. Bn placed in ~~Reserve~~ Divisional Reserve + ready to move at one hours notice.	R.H.R.W.
EASTWOOD CAMP. HAVRINCOURT WOOD.	24/2/18		O.C. Bn, Adjutant, and one officer per Coy reconnoitred the back areas of the Divisional front with a view to carrying out instructions laid down in the Division + Bde. defence scheme. C of E. parade service held under cover of the wood. 1 O.R. proceeded on leave.	R.H.R.W.
ditto	25/2/18		Bn worked on improving the camp. During the forenoon camp was visited by the Divisional who expressed his approval of work in progress. Work commenced under R E supervision.	R.H.R.W.

A7092). Wt. W12839/M1297 750,000. 1/17. D. D & L., Ltd. Forms/C2118/14.

Instructions regarding War Diaries and Intelligence Summaries are contained in F. S. Regs., Part II. and the Staff Manual respectively. Title pages will be prepared in manuscript.

WAR DIARY
or
~~INTELLIGENCE SUMMARY.~~
(Erase heading not required.)

Army Form C. 2118.

Place	Date	Hour	Summary of Events and Information	Remarks and references to Appendices
EASTWOOD CAMP HAVRINCOURT WOOD.	26/2/18.		2 officers Lt. MIDDLETON + 2nd Lt. HOLLOWAY, + 50 O.R.s joined Bn. Lt. Middleton resumed the duties of Transport officer vice 2nd Lt. Gilbert to "A" Coy. 2nd Lt Holloway to D Coy. Operation Order no. 185 for relief on night of 27th/28th received. Sentence of Ch/18716 Pte J. Chemmings commuted to 5 years Penal servitude by order of the Army Commander.	RMH.
ditto.	27/2/18		Coys at the disposal of O.C. Companies. All Blankets packs + etc. returned to stores in preparation for line. Ch/190.S. Pte. H. Pike handed over to A.P.M for safe custody during period in the line. EASTWOOD camp turned over to advance party of 2nd Bn RMLI at 4.30 P.M. At 5 P.M Bn entrained at EASTWOOD camp Light Railway station detraining at TRESCAULT at 5.30 P.M. the Bn proceeded by overland track to SUPPORT trenches, relief of ANSON Bn completed at 8.30 P.M.	RMH.
SUPPORT Trench FLESQUIERES.	28/2/18.		T/Surgeon H.C. Broadhurst joined Bn + relieved Capt. H.C. [illegible] RAMC. 148th F.A. 3 N.C.O.s + 30 O.R.s employed on Digging Bde H.Q. TRESCAULT [illegible] at 9 A.M. 6 officers 16 N.C.O.s ~~[illegible]~~ and 200 O.R.s employed on [illegible] work digging immediate SUPPORT line to FRONTLINE task consisted of excavating 4 ft at top + 3 ft deep + 3 ft at bottom, commenced at about 6.15 P.M. finished at 10.30 P.M. [illegible] E.A. forced to [illegible] through effect of M.G. + L.G. fire. Enemy [illegible] normal. Wind [illegible] changing to North. Slight rain + hail showers intermittently. [illegible] good.	RMH

CKFletcher
Lieut-Colonel RMLI

A7092). Wt. W12839/M1297 750,000. 1/17. D. D & L., Ltd. Forms/C2118/14.

188th Brigade.

63rd Division.

1st BATTALION

ROYAL MARINE LIGHT INFANTRY

M A R C H 1 9 1 8

CONFIDENTIAL.

188
63

W A R D I A R Y

of

1st BATTALION, ROYAL MARINES.

VOLUME XXI.

- From -

1st MARCH, 1918,

- To -

31st MARCH, 1918.

R. H. [illegible]
Captain

for Lieut.-Colonel, R.M.L.I.,
Commanding 1st Batta lion, Royal Marines.

22

To :-

1/Bn. Royal Marines

Instructions regarding War Diaries and Intelligence Summaries are contained in F. S. Regs., Part II. and the Staff Manual respectively. Title pages will be prepared in manuscript.

WAR DIARY
or
~~INTELLIGENCE SUMMARY.~~
(Erase heading not required.)

Army Form C. 2118.

Sheet P. 1

Place	Date	Hour	Summary of Events and Information	Remarks and references to Appendices
RIBECOURT LEFT In Support.	1/3/18.		Bn in Support to ANSON Bn. 2 Coys in SCREW TRENCH and KAISER TRENCH. 1 Coy in CHAPEL WOOD SWITCH remaining Coy in SCREW TRENCH	[illegible]
ditto.	2/3/18.		Operation Order No. 86 issued for Relief Bn by 2nd Bn R.M.L.I. and for Relief of ANSON Bn on night of 3rd/4th.	R.H.M.
ditto	3/3/18		Bn was relieved by 2nd Bn R.M.L.I. at 7.30 P.M. On completion of relief Bn relieved ANSON Bn in FRONT LINE, relief completed about 10.30 P.M.	R.H.P.M.
RIBECOURT LEFT. FRONT LINE	4/3/18.		Situation remained unchanged and casualties slight. Bn employed during night completing "T" head posts, revetting and clearing communication trenches.	R.H.P.M.
ditto	5/3/18.		ditto. ditto.	R.H.P.M.
"	6/3/18		Operation Order No. 87 ~~[illegible]~~ for Relief of Bn by 2nd Bn R.M.L.I. issued. Situation remained unchanged and casualties ~~light~~ nil very slight.	R.H.P.M.
"	7/3/18		2nd Bn R.M.L.I. relieved Bn on night of 7th relief completed at 11.30 P.M. On completion of relief Bn moved to EASTWOOD Camp, entraining at TRESCAULT detraining at Station B.W. 19.	R.H.P.M.

A5834 Wt. W4973/M687 750,000 8/16 D. D. & L. Ltd. Forms/C.2118/13.

Instructions regarding War Diaries and Intelligence Summaries are contained in F. S. Regs., Part II. and the Staff Manual respectively. Title pages will be prepared in manuscript.

1/Bn Royal Marines

WAR DIARY
or
~~INTELLIGENCE SUMMARY.~~
(Erase heading not required.)

Army Form C. 2118.

Sheet No 2.

Place	Date	Hour	Summary of Events and Information	Remarks and references to Appendices
EASTWOOD Camp.	8/3/18		Bn. spent day cleaning up and resting. All S.B.R's inspected and S.A.A. deficiencies completed. Working party of 100 O.R's working in camp ~~and~~ under supervision of WORCESTER PIONEERS. Bn. "Stood to" during forenoon.	R.H.P.W.
ditto.	9/3/18.		Training and practices for raid carried out in forenoon. Working parties for M.T.M's, and WORCESTER PIONEERS supplied also working party of 2 officers and 250 O.R's working on BURIED CABLE. SUMMER TIME came into force at 12 mid-night.	R.H.P.W.
ditto.	10/3/18.		Bn Operation Order No. 88 issued for relieving ANSON Bn in SUPPORT on night of 11th/12th. Working parties as for 9/3/18 supplied.	R.H.P.W.
ditto	11/3/18.		Bn relieved ANSON Bn in SUPPORT relief completed by 11 P.M. During relief Bn was heavily GAS shelled passing through TRESCAULT. Casualties 2 Officers 40 O.R's.	R.H.P.W.
~~SUPPORT~~ SUPPORT. in GRAND RAVINE.	12/3/18		Three Coys. in GRAND RAVINE, B Coy in SCREW TRENCH at disposal of O.C. FRONT LINE Bn. Day spent in clearing RAVINE, and DUGOUTS, of GAS. Working Parties supplied for work under R.E's on the BILHELM CHAPEL WOOD SWITCH and the BROWN LINE. Area heavily shelled at night with GAS SHELLS.	R.H.P.W.
ditto.	13/3/18		Usual working parties supplied on BROWN LINE and BILHELM CHAPEL WOOD SWITCH. Intermittent shelling of GRAND RAVINE during night with GAS SHELL.	R.H.P.W.

A5834 Wt. W4973/M687 750,000 8/16 D. D. & L. Ltd. Forms/C.2118/13.

1/Bn Royal Marines

WAR DIARY
or
~~INTELLIGENCE SUMMARY.~~
(*Erase heading not required.*)

Army Form C. 2118.

Sheet No 3

Instructions regarding War Diaries and Intelligence Summaries are contained in F. S. Regs., Part II. and the Staff Manual respectively. Title pages will be prepared in manuscript.

Place	Date	Hour	Summary of Events and Information	Remarks and references to Appendices
~~[illegible]~~ Bn in SUPPORT GRAND RAVINE.	14/3/18.		Usual working parties under R.E^s supplied. Orders received for re-organisation of reliefs. 100 O.R^s received from NELSON Bn.	R.A.P.W.
ditto.	15/3/18		Coy under disposal of O.C. FRONTLINE Bn ceased work on BILHELM CHAPEL WOOD SWITCH working on SHEREWOOD SWITCH at night. Remaining 3 coys worked under RE supervision on BROWN LINE and CHAPEL WOOD SWITCH	R.H.P.W.
ditto.	16/3/18		One Coy working on SHEREWOOD SWITCH at night, 2 Coys under RE^s during day, remaining coy working under STAFF CAPTAIN establishing ammunition dumps in HAVRINCOURT defences, BROWN LINE and CHAPEL WOOD SWITCH. Intermittent GAS SHELLING at night	R.H.P.W
ditto	17/3/18		As for 16/3/18.	
ditto.	18/3/18		Bn Operation order no. 89 for relief of 2nd Bn R.M.L.I in FRONT LINE issued. Work as for 16th and 17th carried out. GRAND RAVINE was again GAS SHELLED during night and BROWN LINE shelled with H.E. during day.	R.H.P.W.
ditto.	19/3/18.		Bn relieved 2nd Bn R.M.L.I in FRONT LINE relief completed about 10 P.M. Bn rested during day	R.H.P.W.

A5834 Wt. W4973/M687 750,000 8/16 D. D. & L. Ltd. Forms/C.2118/13.

1/Bn Royal Marines

WAR DIARY
or
~~INTELLIGENCE SUMMARY~~
(Erase heading not required.)

Army Form C. 2118

Sheet No 4

Instructions regarding War Diaries and Intelligence Summaries are contained in F. S. Regs., Part II. and the Staff Manual respectively. Title Pages will be prepared in manuscript.

Place	Date	Hour	Summary of Events and Information	Remarks and references to Appendices
~~21/3/18~~. FRONTLINE BN HQ SCREWTRENCH	20/3/18		Usual trench routine carried out during day. All posts & front line were freed of MUD & WATER. At night PATROLS were pushed forward & gaps in wire filled up. ~~Orders received to evacuate and HAVRINCOURT defences. Evacuation completed and positions taken up before dawn. Bn HQ established in HAVRINCOURT WOOD.~~	RAS Crapper Lt.
~~[illegible]~~ ditto,	21/3/18		FRONT LINE and back area heavily shelled during early morning, & intermittent shelling during day.	
FLESQUIERES			Battn: ordered to withdraw through 2nd Bn. R.M.L.I, thereby causing SUPPORT LINE to become FRONT LINE.	RAS Crapper Lt.
HAVRINCOURT WOOD.	22/3/18		Bn: ordered to evacuate & proceed to OLD BRITISH LINE in HAVRINCOURT WOOD. Shortly before evacuation, Lt. Colonel C.J. Farquharson M.C. RMLI commanding 2nd Bn R.M.L.I. wounded in BROWN LINE.	RAS Crapper Lt.
	23/3/18		Battn: proceeded to prepared line in front of BERTINCOURT & took up position in FRONT LINE on the left of 2nd Bn. RMLI. During the afternoon enemy heavily shelled the right Battn:	

Cont'd

1/Bn. Royal Marines

Instructions regarding War Diaries and Intelligence Summaries are contained in F. S. Regs., Part II. and the Staff Manual respectively. Title pages will be prepared in manuscript.

WAR DIARY

~~or~~

~~INTELLIGENCE SUMMARY.~~

(Erase heading not required.)

Army Form C. 2118.

Sheet No 5

Place	Date	Hour	Summary of Events and Information	Remarks and references to Appendices
BETINCOURT	24/3/18		Bn. ordered to withdraw from BERTINCOURT & proceed to BAPAUME - PERONNE ROAD thence to MARTINPUICH.	[illegible] Lt.
MARTINPUICH	25/3/18		Bn. in conjunction with remainder of Bde, fought rearguard action to THIEPVAL, where Bde. took up a position & remained there during the night 25/26th/3/18.	[illegible] Lt.
THIEPVAL	26/3/18		Ordered to Withdraw across RIVER ANCRE to HAMEL, where the Battn. took up a defensive position. Relieved by 1Bn. The Queens & proceeded to MARTINSART into billets	[illegible] Lt.
			Contd.	

D. D. & L., London, E.C.
(A8001) Wt. W1771/M2031 750,000 5/17 Sch. 52 Forms/C2118/14

1/Bn Royal Marines

Instructions regarding War Diaries and Intelligence Summaries are contained in F. S. Regs., Part II. and the Staff Manual respectively. Title pages will be prepared in manuscript.

WAR DIARY

~~or~~

~~INTELLIGENCE SUMMARY.~~

(Erase heading not required.)

Army Form C. 2118.

Sheet No 6.

Place	Date	Hour	Summary of Events and Information	Remarks and references to Appendices
MARTINSART	27/3/18		During the night enemy patrols pushed through MESNIL + N end of AVELUY WOOD. A general counter attack was made in order to clear MESNIL + N. end of WOOD in with 2 Companies of this battalion took part.	[illegible]
AVELUY WOOD.	28/3/18		Relieved & proceeded to ~~MAILLET~~ MAILLET & thence later in the day to FORCEVILLE into rest billets.	[illegible]
FORCEVILLE	29/3/18		Reorganizing etc etc	[illegible]
"	30/3/18		" " Bn. inspected by G.O.C. 188th Inf Bde.	[illegible]
"	31/3/18		" " Church parades etc.	[illegible]
			Casualties during operations 22.3.18 – 28.3.18 inclusive – were:–	
			KILLED: Offs 1, ORs 20; WOUNDED: Offs 5, ORs 78; MISSING: Offs 7, ORs 337	

[illegible] Lieut Colonel R.M.L.I. Comdg 1st Bn Royal Marines

D. D. & L., London, E.C. (A8001) Wt. W1771/M2031 750,000 5/17 Sch. 52 Forms/C2118/14

188th Inf.Bde.
63rd Div.

WAR DIARY

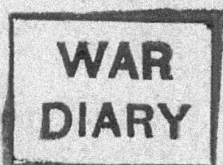

1st BATTN. THE ROYAL MARINE LIGHT INFANTRY.

A P R I L

1 9 1 8

SECRET

CONFIDENTIAL.

WAR DIARY

— of —

1st Bn. Royal Marine Light Infantry

Volume 22

— from —

April 1st 1918

— to —

April 30th 1918

WD 21

To. H.Qrs 63rd R.N. Division

E.K. Fletcher

Lieut. Colonel R.M.L.I.

Comdg 1st Bn. R.M.L.I.

Instructions regarding War Diaries and Intelligence Summaries are contained in F. S. Regs., Part II. and the Staff Manual respectively. Title Pages will be prepared in manuscript.

WAR DIARY
or
INTELLIGENCE SUMMARY
(Erase heading not required.)

Army Form C. 2118

Place	Date	Hour	Summary of Events and Information	Remarks and references to Appendices
FORCEVILLE.	1/4/18.		Bn billeted in VILLAGE. Training and reorganisation commenced in the morning. Three parties of 1 officer and 50. O.R's employed on night digging leaving VILLAGE at 5.45 P.M returning 12.15 AM. Warning order for Bn to move to TOOTENCOURT received.	RHW.
ditto.	2/4/18.		Bn moved by route march to TOOTENCOURT leaving FORCEVILLE at 12.10 P.M. arriving TOOTENCOURT at about 3 P.M. Accommodation was found to be lacking. Bn eventually placed in Y.M.C.A hut and R.F.C hangar. Warning order received for Bde to move and hold the line again.	RHW
~~ditto~~ ENGLEBELMER	3/4/18		In accordance with instructions Bn moved from TOOTENCOURT by Route March to ENGLEBELMER. Bde in reserve to 190th Inf Bde. Bn Bivouaced in orchards outside village. Bn H.Q established in village at Q 19. d. 7.7. Intermittent shelling of village and surroundings during day and night. LIEUT-COL. E.K. FLETCHER assumed command of the Bn. MAJOR. N.S. CLUTTERBUCK took over command of 2/R.M.L.I.	RHW.
ditto	4/4/18		80 O.R's proceeded on signal course. 5 officers of MIDDLESEX ENTRENCHING Bn joined Bn. VILLAGE and BIVOUACS intermittently shelled throughout day. Casualties NIL.	R.HW.

1875 Wt. W593/826 1,000,000 4/15 J.B.C. & A. A.D.S.S./Forms/C. 2118.

Army Form C. 2118.

Instructions regarding War Diaries and Intelligence Summaries are contained in F. S. Regs., Part II. and the Staff Manual respectively. Title pages will be prepared in manuscript.

WAR DIARY
or
INTELLIGENCE SUMMARY.

(Erase heading not required.)

Place	Date	Hour	Summary of Events and Information	Remarks and references to Appendices
ENGLEBELMER	5/4/18		Heavy bombardment of village and surroundings with H.E. and a few gas shells, amongst latter several 'Blue Cross', commencing at 4-0 A.M. and continuing all day.	
		1-30P.M.	The Bn. was placed at the disposal of the G.O.C. 190th Infantry Brigade, holding the Front line. 'A' COY. CAPT. CAMPBELL. moved up in support of 7th Bn.	
AVELUY WOOD		3-0P.M.	ROYAL FUSILIERS, and was followed by H.Q. and 'B' COY. The situation in the WOOD at this time was obscure. Patrols discovered two gaps in the Line, which	
	6/4/18	7-0P.M.	were filled. After mixed fighting during the night a defensive flank was formed with LEFT of 24th LONDON. 47th DIVISION. In this fighting following Officers became casualties. KILLED. LT. G.J. WHARF. R.M.L.I. WOUNDED. 2/LIEUTS. PERRY and SHIMOLD. MIDDLESEX REGT.	
do.		7-45A.M.	2/R.M.L.I. arrived in support. At 9-30 A.M. a counter-attack by 2/R.M.L.I., assisted by 1/R.M.L.I. was successful in re-establishing original FRONT LINE. Contact was obtained with 4th BEDFORD on our LEFT. Line was consolidated under heavy shell fire, and both Bns. re-organised with 1/R.M.L.I. on RIGHT and 2/R.M.L.I. on LEFT. Enemy aeroplanes were active during the afternoon, dropping lights along our line of Posts. In the counter-attack 55 Prisoners and 10 M.G. were captured. Remaining details of ROYAL FUSILIERS were withdrawn after dark.	

D. D. & L., London, E.C. (A6004) Wt. W1771/M2031 750,000 5/17 Sch. 52 Forms/C2118/14

Instructions regarding War Diaries and Intelligence Summaries are contained in F. S. Regs., Part II. and the Staff Manual respectively. Title pages will be prepared in manuscript.

WAR DIARY
or
INTELLIGENCE SUMMARY.
(Erase heading not required.)

Army Form C. 2118.

Place	Date	Hour	Summary of Events and Information	Remarks and references to Appendices
AVELUY WOOD	7/4/18		2/LTS. BIRBER, + SPRAGON, MIDDLESEX REGT, 2/LT. DARK, R.W. KENTS + TREGEDGA, R.M. wounded. Battalion relieved by ANSON BATTALION, returning to billets in FORCEVILLE, arriving 6 a.m. 8/4/18.	R.H.M.
FORCEVILLE	8/4/18		The following officers + o.r. joined the Battalion: Capt. R. POLAND, from hospital 2nd in command, 10 officers and 265 o.r. MIDDLESEX REGT, and 40 o.r. R.M.L.I. Batt. re-organised in four companies, commanded as follows:- A Coy, CAPT. WALTER, MIDDLESEX REGT; B Coy CAPT. R. CAMPBELL R.M.L.I.; 'C' Coy 2/LT HORNE, R.M.; 'D' Coy LT. HOTHAM, R.M.	R.H.M.
do	9/4/18		Battalion relieved ANSON BATTALION in AVELUY WOOD.	
AVELUY WOOD	10/4/18		Fairly quiet. Some M.G. and Minnenwerfer activity. 4 o.r. to L.T.M. course.	
	11/4/18		Bn. digging in, in AVELUY WOOD. 2/LT. E. ATTWATER, MIDDLESEX REGT. wounded. Bn. relieved by ARTISTS RIFLES, and returned to billets in FORCEVILLE arriving 3 a.m. 12/4/18.	R.H.M.
FORCEVILLE	12/4/18		Battalion resting at FORCEVILLE. 'D' Company bathed and received clean clothing. 54 o.r. R.M.L.I. arrived. SUB-LIEUT. NEIL, HOWE Bn, rejoined.	
	13/4/18		Bn. reorganised with four platoons per company. Some training done. Remainder of Battalion bathed. Lewis Gunners to L.G. instruction.	R.H.M.

Army Form C. 2118

Instructions regarding War Diaries and Intelligence Summaries are contained in F. S. Regs., Part II. and the Staff Manual respectively. Title Pages will be prepared in manuscript.

WAR DIARY
or
INTELLIGENCE SUMMARY
(Erase heading not required.)

Place	Date	Hour	Summary of Events and Information	Remarks and references to Appendices
ARQUEVES,	14/4/18.		Bn. moved to ARQUEVES by route march. Headquarters at O.14.a.8.1.	
do.	15/4/18.		Party of 250 men for work on CORPS LINE. Lewis Gunners & Signallers training under L.G.O. & S.O.	RHW
do	16/4/18.		Party for work on CORPS LINE. Lt. D. M. SMITH, R.M. joined from ENGLAND. - to "B" Company.	
do	17/4/18		Battalion at Company training.	
do	18/4/18		Battalion at Company training.	
do	19/4/18.		350 men for work on CORPS LINE. Lecture and demonstration on artillery formation by the G.O.C. to the officers of the Brigade. Lewis Gunners to instruction under L.G.O. Major F.B.A. LAWRIE joined from BASE DEPOT to H.Q.	RHW
do	20/4/18.		Bn. practised advance in artillery formation on 1000x front. M.M. awarded to Ch/19534. Cpl (A/Sgt) G.W. PARKES.	
do	21/4/18.		Joint Church Parade of 1/R.M.L.I. & 2/R.M.L.I. at O.20.a.3.6.	
do.	22/4/18.		Demonstration of "blood on the billet" musketry training by MAJOR I. BOSTOCK, K.O.Y.L.I. 3rd ARMY MUSKETRY SCH. 5.15 Lecture & demonstration by MAJOR BOSTOCK. The following officers joined from ENGLAND:- LTS. R.A. MC.BRYDE, G.P. MASCALL; 2/LTS. MATTHEWS; A.E. CREED; J.D. STEELE; J.A. CORRAN; E.A. BRINDLEY; T.G. STEWART; A.W. GREGORY; F. BRUNNELL.	RHW.
	23/4/18.		300 men for work on CORPS LINE. CAPT. J.A. THOMAS, R.M. joined from ENGLAND.	

Instructions regarding War Diaries and Intelligence Summaries are contained in F. S. Regs., Part II. and the Staff Manual respectively. Title pages will be prepared in manuscript.

WAR DIARY
or
~~INTELLIGENCE~~ SUMMARY.
(Erase heading not required.)

Army Form C. 2118.

Place	Date	Hour	Summary of Events and Information	Remarks and references to Appendices
ARQUEVES	21/4/18 ~~22/4/18~~		Bn. at Coy. training. Training & bathing. The following officers awarded the Military Cross:- Temp/Captain R. H. W. West, Temp/Lieut. G. J. Wharf, Temp/Lieut. J. W. Middleton all R.M.L.I.	RHW
"	25/4/18		Bn. at Coy training. T/Capt. J. Thomas joined Battn. from Base Depot 22/4/18 & posted to B Coy.	
"	26/4/18		Working party & Coy training. The following message sent to the 4th Battn Royal Marines:- "To the Officers, W.Os NCOs & men of the 4th Battn Royal Marines" — "Heartiest congratulations from the Officers, W.Os NCOs & men of the 1st Bn. Royal Marines."	RHW
"	~~[illegible]~~ 27/4/18		Church Parade. Honours & Awards (D.R.O. 3973) The Field Marshall Commander-in-Chief has, under authority granted by His Majesty the King, awards & decorations as under:-	RHW
			The Distinguished Service Order Major (A/Lt. Colonel) F. K. Fletcher 1st Bn. R.M.L.I. Major (A/Lt. Colonel) H. S. Clutterbuck 2nd Bn. R.M.L.I.	
			The Undermentioned NCOs & men have been awarded the Military Medal:- Po/652/S Cpl. E. Beresford 1/RMLI Ch/18167 Pte. E. J. Mell WZ 342 P.O. E. O. Evans att.d HOWE BATT.N Ply/1093/S L/Cpl. E. Holway 1/RMLI "/12885 Cpl (A Sgt) D. O. B. West	RHW
			The Army, Corps, Divisional, Brigade & Battn. Commanders congratulate the recipients	

(A7092). Wt W12839/M1293 75,0c0. 1/17. D. D. & L., Ltd. Forms/C.2118/14.

Army Form C. 2118.

Instructions regarding War Diaries and Intelligence Summaries are contained in F. S. Regs., Part II. and the Staff Manual respectively. Title pages will be prepared in manuscript.

WAR DIARY
or
INTELLIGENCE SUMMARY.

(Erase heading not required.)

Place	Date	Hour	Summary of Events and Information	Remarks and references to Appendices
ARQUEVES	28/4/18		Reorganization. The 1st Bn. R.M.L.I. & the 2nd Bn. R.M.L.I. will be amalgamated tomorrow 29/4/18 & will be known as the 1st Bn. Royal Marines. Company training.	[illegible]
"	29/4/18		Companies in the attack	
"	30/4/18		Specialist Training. A working party of 300 workers marched to rendezvous & worked on PAS - YARDENCOURT defences. The undermentioned officers have been struck off the strength of this Bn & transferred to England. Revd E E Farquharson RM (S) 2nd Lt C H Bailey (W)	[illegible]

C W Fletcher

Lieut. Colonel RMLI

Comdg 1st Bn Royal Marines

D. D. & L., London, E.C. (A8001) Wt. W1771/M2031 750,000 5/17 Sch. 52 Forms/C2118/14

CONFIDENTIAL.

W A R   D I A R Y

of

1st BATTALION, ROYAL MARINES.

VOLUME XXIII.

- FROM -

1st MAY, 1918,

- TO -

31st MAY, 1918.

R H West

Capt & adjt.

for Lieut. -Colonel, R.M.L.I.,

Commanding 1st Battalion, Royal Marines.

Vol 24

To:-

1/Bn Royal Marines

Army Form C. 2118.

Sheet No. 1

Instructions regarding War Diaries and Intelligence Summaries are contained in F. S. Regs., Part II. and the Staff Manual respectively. Title pages will be prepared in manuscript.

WAR DIARY
or
INTELLIGENCE SUMMARY.

(Erase heading not required.)

Place	Date	Hour	Summary of Events and Information	Remarks and references to Appendices
[illegible] ARQUEVES	1/5/18		Company Training	R.A. Sprague Lt
	2/5/18		Company Training	R.A. Sprague Lt
	3/5/18		250 O.R.s worked on PAS - VADENCOURT LINE	R.A. Sprague Lt
			Honours & awards. The Field Marshall Commander in Chief has under authority granted by His Majesty the King awarded the Military Medal to the undermentioned NCOs & men	
			Ply/827/S Cpl J. LARTER 2nd Bn RMLI att'd Y/63rd T.M.B.	
			Po/17741 Pte N. ARTIS	
			Po/17183 Sgt H. TRUSSLER 2nd Bn RMLI	
			Ply/13642 Sgt (A/C.S.M.) W.D. Croke	
			Ply/11352 Pte (A/Sgt) H.S. McCULLOUGH 2nd Bn RMLI	
			Ply/13941 Sgt J. J. McCORMACK	
			Ply/11929 Cpl (A/Sgt) J. KISSOCK	
			Po/1500 Pte G. MARSHALL	
			Po/16832 Pte A.S. GREEN	
			Ply/1068 Pte G.W. BELL	
			The Army, Corps, Divisional, Brigade & Batt'n Commanders congratulate the recipients.	
			Cont'd	

D. D. & L., London, E.C.
(A5004) Wt. W1771/M2031 750,000 5/17 Sch. 52 Forms/C2118/14

Instructions regarding War Diaries and Intelligence Summaries are contained in F. S. Regs., Part II. and the Staff Manual respectively. Title pages will be prepared in manuscript.

1/Bn Royal Marines

WAR DIARY
or
INTELLIGENCE SUMMARY.
(Erase heading not required.)

Army Form C. 2118.

Vol. 2

Place	Date	Hour	Summary of Events and Information	Remarks and references to Appendices
ARCQUEUES	3/5/18.		Contd	[illegible]
			NOTICE:- The following has been received from the 4th Battn Royal Marines, in reply to the message sent by the Officers, W.O.s N.C.O.s & men of the 1st Bn & 2nd Bns R.M.L.I. "Very many thanks for your kind congratulations which are much appreciated by all ranks"	
			4th Battn Royal Marines.	
			The following congratulatory messages have been received & sent:—	
			From Vice Admiral Sir Roger Keyes C.B. CMG M.V.O DSO R.N	
			To G.O.C. 63rd (RN) Division:	
			"Greetings on Glorious 25th April from KEYES"	
			From General Lawrie & Royal Naval Division.	
			To Vice Admiral Keyes, Dover.	
			Greetings reciprocated with our united congratulations on your splendid success.	
			Contd	

D. D. & L., London, E.C. (A8001) Wt. W1771/M2031 750,000 5/17 Sch. 52 Forms/C2118/14

Instructions regarding War Diaries and Intelligence Summaries are contained in F. S. Regs., Part II. and the Staff Manual respectively. Title pages will be prepared in manuscript.

1/Bn Royal Marines

WAR DIARY
or
INTELLIGENCE SUMMARY.

(Erase heading not required.)

Army Form C. 2118.

Sheet No 3

Place	Date	Hour	Summary of Events and Information	Remarks and references to Appendices
do. FARQUEVES	3/5/18		Contd.	R.W. Spragge Lt. Col.
			NOTICE contd. From Vice Admiral Keyes.	
			To General Lawrie, Royal Naval Division B.E.F.	
			"On behalf of the Forces I had the great honour to command on St George's Day. I wish to tell you that we are very proud to have received such a message from the Royal Naval Division."	
"	4/5/18		Divine Service. 250 workers marched to & worked on the FORCEVILLE LINE.	R.W. Spragge Lt. Col.
	5/5/18		Company training.	R.W. Spragge Lt. Col.
	6/5/18		Honours & awards:- The Field Marshall, Commander-in-Chief has under authority granted by His Majesty the King, awarded decorations as under:- The Military Cross	R.W. Spragge Lt. Col.
			Capt. R.A. Campbell R.M.L.I.	
			2/2nd Lt. C.H. Baley R.M.	
			Lt. W. Spragon Middlesex Regt.	
			The G.O.C. Divisional Brigade & Batt. Commanders congratulate the recipients.	Contd.

D. D. & L., London, E.C. (A8001) Wt. W1771/M2031 750,000 5/17 Sch. 52 Forms/C2118/14

Instructions regarding War Diaries and Intelligence Summaries are contained in F. S. Regs., Part II. and the Staff Manual respectively. Title pages will be prepared in manuscript.

1/Bn Royal Marines

WAR DIARY
or
~~INTELLIGENCE SUMMARY.~~
(Erase heading not required.)

Army Form C. 2118.

Sheet No 4

Place	Date	Hour	Summary of Events and Information	Remarks and references to Appendices
ARCQUEVES	6/5/18		Contd. The Lords Commissioners of the Admiralty has approved of the undermentioned Temp. 2nd Lieuts. Royal Marines, being promoted to the rank of Temp/Lieut Royal Marines from the date stated against their names:–	[illegible]
			T.E. WRIGHT 26th Apl/1918 — C.E. MENNELL 26th Apl/1918	
			H.H. HARPER " — E. WILKS "	
			F.C. HOWE " — F.H. BRETTELL "	
			J.V. LORD " — C.V. EGAN "	
			C.L.C. McKEAND " — W.C. WILLIAMSON MC "	
			E.D. BARNARD " — H.J. WILCOX "	
			H.G. BENNETT "	
	7/5/18		Company inspections etc prior to proceeding up the line.	[illegible]
	7/5/18 / 8/5/18	night	Battalion relieved the 2nd Batt. the [illegible] Regiment in support on front of HAMEL	[illegible]

Contd.

1/Bn Royal Marines

WAR DIARY
or
INTELLIGENCE SUMMARY.
(Erase heading not required.)

Instructions regarding War Diaries and Intelligence Summaries are contained in F. S. Regs., Part II. and the Staff Manual respectively. Title pages will be prepared in manuscript.

Army Form C. 2118.

Sheet No 5

Place	Date	Hour	Summary of Events and Information	Remarks and references to Appendices
SUPPORT in front of HAMEL	8/5/18		Front quiet.	[signature]
"	9/5/18		Our artillery fairly active. During the night Battn worked on intermediate system.	[signature]
"	10/5/18		General inactivity prevailed. Wiring & digging parties worked on intermediate system & RIDGE TRENCH (close support to front line).	[signature]
"	11/5/18		Intermittent artillery fire carried out by both sides. Digging & wiring continued with during night on RIDGE TRENCH, & CHARLES AVENUE cleared of [illegible] & fire steps constructed at intervals for use in conjunction with left flank defences. Chain of strong points built up from CLOSE SUPPORT to INTERMEDIATE LINE.	[signature]
"	12/5/18		Front fairly quiet. Continued work on chain of strong points.	[signature]
"	13/5/18		Our artillery considerably active on back areas.	[signature]
"	13/5/18 night / 14/5/18		Battn relieved ANZAC BATTn in front line in front of HAMEL.	[signature]

D. D. & L., London, E.C. (A8001) Wt. W1771/M2031 750,000 5/17 Sch. 52 Forms/C2118/14

Instructions regarding War Diaries and Intelligence Summaries are contained in F. S. Regs., Part II. and the Staff Manual respectively. Title pages will be prepared in manuscript.

1/Bn Royal Marines

WAR DIARY

or

~~INTELLIGENCE SUMMARY.~~

(Erase heading not required.)

Army Form C. 2118.

Place	Date	Hour	Summary of Events and Information	Remarks and references to Appendices
FRONTLINE before HAMEL	14/5/18		Our artillery considerably active on BEAUCOURT – MIRAUMONT ROAD. Enemy transport blown up. During afternoon small parties of the enemy seen [illegible] up [illegible] away the horseflesh.	[illegible]
"	15/5/18		Morning quiet. During the afternoon enemy shelled the left of our front line but without effect. We had no casualties.	[illegible]
"	16/5/18		Activity normal.	[illegible]
"	17/5/18		At 6 a.m. Enemy shelled CLOSE SUPPORT (RIDGE TRENCH) from centre to NORTHERN BOUNDARY, damage done to trench practically NIL. We had no casualties. During the night front line coys ~~[illegible]~~ posts for all round defence.	[illegible]
"	18/5/18		Nothing of importance happened throughout the day.	[illegible]

D. D. & L., London, E.C. (A8094) Wt. W1771/M2031 750,000 5/17 Sch. 52 Forms/C2118/14

1/Bn Royal Marines

WAR DIARY
or
INTELLIGENCE SUMMARY.
(*Erase heading not required.*)

Army Form C. 2118.

Sheet No 7

Instructions regarding War Diaries and Intelligence Summaries are contained in F. S. Regs., Part II. and the Staff Manual respectively. Title pages will be prepared in manuscript.

Place	Date	Hour	Summary of Events and Information	Remarks and references to Appendices
FRONT LINE HAMEL SECTOR LEFT	18-5-18 } 19-5-18 }	night of	On the night of 18th–19th May "C" Coy of the Battn in conjunction with HAWKE Battn on the right raided the enemy outpost positions in the HAMEL SECTOR. ZERO HOUR 12.15 A.M. At 12.15 A.M. 11.5" How, 18 Pdr, H.T.Ms, M.T.Ms & L.T.Ms opened up & at ZERO + 3 the raiders advanced towards their objectives. When the objective was reached it was found to have been recently evacuated by the enemy, & unfortunately we were unable to obtain identification of any kind. Dugouts & shelters were effectively bombed [illegible] after being raided & much damage was done. At ZERO + 32 the raiders returned. Our casualties were remarkably small & included 2nd Lt [illegible] who was slightly wounded [illegible] slightly wounded [illegible] the latter remaining at duty.	[illegible]

D. D. & L., London, E.C. (A8004) Wt. W1771/M2031 750,000 5/17 Sch. 52 Forms/C2118/14

1/Bn Royal Marines

Instructions regarding War Diaries and Intelligence Summaries are contained in F. S. Regs., Part II. and the Staff Manual respectively. Title pages will be prepared in manuscript.

WAR DIARY
or
INTELLIGENCE SUMMARY.
(Erase heading not required.)

Army Form C. 2118.

Sheet No. 8

Place	Date	Hour	Summary of Events and Information	Remarks and references to Appendices
FRONT LINE before HAMEL	19/5/18		Normal activity. Surgeon A Rane-Gould instantly killed whilst standing outside SICK BAY by enemy shell	[illegible]
			2nd Royal Irish Regt relieved Battn in front line.	
	19/5/18 – 20/5/18	night of	Battalion moved back into reserve at FORCEVILLE – 1 Company remaining in ENGLEBELMER LINE which was our line of resistance in case of attack.	[illegible]
FORCEVILLE	20/5/18		~~[illegible]~~ Company Training carried out	
			Honours & awards. – The Field Marshall Commander in Chief has, under authority granted by His Majesty the King, awarded decorations as under:–	
			Bar to Military Cross. T/Capt G.A. NEWLING M.C. R.M.L.I. 1st Bn	
			The Military Cross. A/Capt R.H. VANCE R.M.L.I. Bn	
			T/Lieut H.R. SMITH R.W. KENT REGT. att'd R.M.L.I. Bn	
			Promotion. The Lords Commissioners of the Admiralty have approved of Lieut, T/Capt. T.H. BURTON M.C. R.M. being promoted to the rank of Captain R.M. from the 23rd April 1918.	
			Contd	

D. D. & L., London, E.C.
(A8001) Wt. W1771/M2031 750,000 5/17 Sch. 52 Forms/C2118/14

Instructions regarding War Diaries and Intelligence Summaries are contained in F. S. Regs., Part II. and the Staff Manual respectively. Title pages will be prepared in manuscript.

1/Bn Royal Marines

WAR DIARY

~~or~~

~~INTELLIGENCE SUMMARY~~

(Erase heading not required.)

Army Form C. 2118.

Sheet No 9

Place	Date	Hour	Summary of Events and Information	Remarks and references to Appendices
FORCEVILLE	20/5/18		NOTICE. The following is to be brought to the notice of every Officer, N.C.O. & man of the ROYAL MARINES.	[illegible] Lieut
			Inspection by H.M. The King, of the depot, Royal Marines, Deal.	
			The Senior Squad of Recruits in future to be known as "The King's Squad".	
			To General White. I am glad to have had an opportunity of inspecting the Depot of the ROYAL MARINES, and I desire to express my entire satisfaction both with the system of training & with the keenness and earnest spirit shown by Officers & men to attain a high standard of war efficiency. It was a pleasure to see the orderly state of the various branches of your depot & I welcome the opportunities given to all ranks for recreation & sport. For some 260 years the ROYAL MARINES have rendered splendid service to the country & during this great war they have had the unique record of taking part in all Naval Actions & of being employed in every theatre of war. Everywhere your Corps has added fresh glory to its record & never has your name stood higher than today. Contd	
			Contd	

D. D. & L., London, E.C. (A8001) Wt. W1771/M2031 750,000 5/17 Sch. 52 Forms/C2118/14

Instructions regarding War Diaries and Intelligence Summaries are contained in F. S. Regs., Part II. and the Staff Manual respectively. Title pages will be prepared in manuscript.

1/Bn Royal Marines

WAR DIARY
or
~~INTELLIGENCE SUMMARY.~~
(Erase heading not required.)

Army Form C. 2118.
Sheet No 10

Place	Date	Hour	Summary of Events and Information	Remarks and references to Appendices
FORCEVILLE	20/5/18		To General White cont^d	
			When you serve on land or afloat remember the achievements of those who have passed through the Depot before you and continue to foster the esprit de corps & fellowship with the Navy which has always been famous in the traditions of the ROYAL MARINES.	[illegible]
			I am prouder than ever to be your Colonel-in-Chief	
			Signed George R.I.	
			7 March. 1918.	
FORCEVILLE	21/5/18		Battn went to Baths & drew clean clothes	[illegible]
			The funeral of the late Surgeon ?? ?? R.N. took place at FORCEVILLE CEMETERY. 1 Officer & 10 O.R. attended.	
"	22/5/18		Company training	
			NOTICE: The following message has been received from the Army Commander: Please convey my congratulations to all ranks of the 63rd R.N. Div? who took part in the successful raid.	[illegible]

D. D. & L., London, E.C.
(A8001) Wt. W1771/M2031 750,000 5/17 Sch. 52 Forms/C2118/14

1/Bn Royal Marines **WAR DIARY** ~~or INTELLIGENCE SUMMARY.~~

(Erase heading not required.)

Instructions regarding War Diaries and Intelligence Summaries are contained in F. S. Regs., Part II. and the Staff Manual respectively. Title pages will be prepared in manuscript.

Army Form C. 2118.

Sheet No 11

Place	Date	Hour	Summary of Events and Information	Remarks and references to Appendices
FORCEVILLE	23/5/18		Company training. During the early hours of the morning Gas alarm sounded. We had no casualties.	
	24/5/18		Companies at disposal of Coy officers	
LINE	25/5/18		[illegible] FRONT LINE in front of HAMEL ~~[illegible]~~	[illegible]
	26/5/18		Quiet. 2 casualties	
	27/5/18		Battn in line 23 reinforcements 3 casualties	[illegible]
	28/5/18		do do One casualty	
	29/5/18		do do 20 reinforcements.	
	30/5/18		Battn moved into support. 19 reinforcements	[illegible]
	31/5/18		Neighbourhood of Bn HQ heavily shelled during morning. 14 reinforcements 3 casualties.	[illegible]

E.K. Fletcher
Lieut Colonel R.M.L.I.
Comdg 1/Bn Royal Marines

D. D. & L., London, E.C. (A8001) Wt. W1771/M2031 750,000 5/17 Sch. 52 Forms/C2118/14

Vol 25

CONFIDENTIAL.

W A R D I A R Y

— of —

1st Battn., ROYAL MARINES.

VOL. XXIV

1st JUNE 1918.

— to —

30th JUNE 1918.

H Horne Lt.
Asst Adjt
for Major. RMLI.,
Commandg 1st Bn., ROYAL MARINES.

Instructions regarding War Diaries and Intelligence Summaries are contained in F. S. Regs., Part II. and the Staff Manual respectively. Title pages will be prepared in manuscript.

WAR DIARY
or
~~INTELLIGENCE SUMMARY.~~
(Erase heading not required.)

Army Form C. 2118.

Place	Date	Hour	Summary of Events and Information	Remarks and references to Appendices
SUPPORT	1/6/18		Normal activity	R.W. Spraggett
"	2/6/18		Near vicinity of H.Q. dugout heavily shelled at intervals throughout the day.	R.W. Spraggett
"	3/6/18		Fairly quiet.	R.W. Spraggett
"	4/6/18		Activity normal	R.W. Spraggett
"	5/6/18		Enemy artillery displayed ~~increasing~~ activity throughout the day.	R.W. Spraggett
"	5/6/18 } 6/6/18 }	NIGHT OF	Battalion relieved & proceeded to V.2.d. in Divisional Reserve.	R.W. Spraggett
V.2.d. map ref. 57c	6/6/18		Battalion employed on digging, also some training was carried out.	R.W. Spraggett
"	7/6/18		" " " " " " " " "	R.W. Spraggett
"	8/6/18		" " " " " " " " "	R.W. Spraggett
"	9/6/18		" " " " " " " " "	R.W. Spraggett
"	10/6/18		" " " " " " " " "	R.W. Spraggett

D. D. & L., London, E.C.
(A8004) Wt. W1771/M2031 750,000 5/17 Sch. 52 Forms/C2118/14

Instructions regarding War Diaries and Intelligence Summaries are contained in F. S. Regs., Part II. and the Staff Manual respectively. Title pages will be prepared in manuscript.

WAR DIARY
~~or~~
~~INTELLIGENCE SUMMARY.~~

(Erase heading not required.)

Army Form C. 2118.

Place	Date	Hour	Summary of Events and Information	Remarks and references to Appendices
V. 2. d.	11/6/18		Battn employed on digging defences: A certain amount of training was also carried out	RW Spragge Lt Col
"	12/6/18		" " " " " " " " "	RW Spragge Lt Col
"	13/6/18		" " " " " " " " "	RW Spragge Lt Col
"	14/6/18		" " " " " " " " "	RW Spragge Lt Col
"	15/6/18		" " " " " & afterwards marched to HERISSART.	RW Spragge Lt Col
HERISSART	16/6/18		Church Parade. At about 11.15 P.M. enemy aircraft flew over & bombs were dropped. Lt Col. C.K. Stephen DSO R.M.L.I. Capt West M.C. R.A.M. being slightly wounded	RW Spragge Lt Col
"	17/6/18		Reorganization of companies etc etc.	RW Spragge Lt Col
"	18/6/18		Company Training	RW Spragge Lt Col
"	19/6/18		Company Training	RW Spragge Lt Col
"	20/6/18		Company Training	RW Spragge Lt Col
"	21/6/18		Battn Sports.	RW Spragge Lt Col
"	22/6/18		Battn employed on wiring defences.	[illegible]

D. D. & L., London, E.C.
(A8001) Wt. W1771/M2031 750,000 5/17 Sch. 52 Forms/C2118/14

Instructions regarding War Diaries and Intelligence Summaries are contained in F. S. Regs., Part II. and the Staff Manual respectively. Title pages will be prepared in manuscript.

WAR DIARY
or
INTELLIGENCE SUMMARY.
(*Erase heading not required.*)

Army Form C. 2118.

Place	Date	Hour	Summary of Events and Information	Remarks and references to Appendices
~~[illegible]~~ ERVE -UMONT- EL SECTOR	23/6/18		Quiet.	R.W. Spraggett Lt.
"	24/6/18		Quiet. Major Sandilands joined Battn. from Wing & assumed the duties of 2nd i/c.	R.W. Spraggett Lt.
"	25/6/18		Activity normal	R.W. Spraggett Lt.
"	26/6/18		Quiet. Lt. Col. E.K. Fletcher DSO RM.L.I. returned from hospital & assumes command this day.	R.W. Spraggett Lt.
"	27/6/18		Quiet	R.W. Spraggett Lt.
"	~~28/6/18~~ 29/6/18		Bn. ~~Quiet~~ L.G.s on range, LIEUT. MCBRIDE rejoins from Bde. reception camp.	R.W. Spraggett Lt.
"	30/6/18		L.G.s on range. CAPT. R.H. CAMPBELL M.C. attd. 188th Infy. Bde for duties of Brigade Major.	[illegible]

D. D. & L., London, E.C.
(A8004) Wt. W1771/M2031 750,000 5/17 Sch. 52 Forms/C2118/14

CONFIDENTIAL.

WAR DIARY

of

1st Battn., ROYAL MARINES.

VOL. XXV

1st JULY 1918

-- to --

31st JULY 1918.

To :- HQ
185th Inf. Bde

A 68

Lieut.Colonel. RMLI,
Commandg 1st Bn., ROYAL MARINES.

Instructions regarding War Diaries and Intelligence Summaries are contained in F. S. Regs., Part II. and the Staff Manual respectively. Title pages will be prepared in manuscript.

WAR DIARY
or
~~INTELLIGENCE SUMMARY.~~
(Erase heading not required.)

Army Form C. 2118.

Place	Date	Hour	Summary of Events and Information	Remarks and references to Appendices
DIVISIONAL RESERVE.	1/7/18.		Battn. provides Working Parties of 5 Off. + 265 O.R. for work with R.E's. LIEUTS. McBRYDE + Hoff reconnoitre FRONT LINE. 2/Lt. MAHDUR SINGH attd. 'D' Coy. for instruction	[illegible]
BEAUMONT-HAMEL SECTOR.	2/7/18		Lewis guns and range. Gas + musketry training. CAPT. E.L. ANDREWS, 2/LTS. SINGH, TURTON + STEELE reconnoitre FRONT LINE.	[illegible]
	3/7/18		250 men for work with R.E's + DIV. SIG. COY.	[illegible]
	4/7/18		150 men for work on BEAUSSART SWITCH, + 100 men for work on new tramway.	
	5/7/18		Battn. preparing for the line. M.O. + I.O. reconnoitre FORWARD ZONE.	[illegible]
	6/7/18		Battn. relieves ARTISTS RIFLES in Adv. Forward Zone.	[illegible]
AUCHONVILLERS	7/7/18		Quiet day. AUCHONVILLERS SHELLED.	[illegible]
	8/7/18		Fairly quiet. Enemy T.M's active.	[illegible]
	9/7/18.		Considerable enemy artillery activity on 'B' Coy.	[illegible]
	10/7/18		Trench mortar activity.	[illegible]
	11/7/18		Quiet. Enemy caught in unexpected relief. Heavily shelled.	[illegible]
	12/7/18		Quiet.	
	13/7/18.		~~Battn~~ Bn. moved into support.	[illegible]
	14/7/18.		Quiet day. AUCHONVILLERS shelled	[illegible]
	15/7/18.		Considerable enemy artillery activity on MAILLY STATION and MILL	[illegible]
SUPPORT BEAUMONT-HAMEL SECTOR.	16/7/18		Fairly quiet.	[illegible]
			Quiet day.	[illegible]
	17/7/18		AUCHONVILLERS shelled intermittently throughout the day. Enemy aircraft attempted to cross our lines and was driven down by A.A. fire. Our artillery active throughout the day.	[illegible]

D. D. & L., London, E.C.
(A8004) Wt. W1771/M2031 750,000 5/17 Sch. 52 Forms/C2118/14

Army Form C. 2118.

Instructions regarding War Diaries and Intelligence Summaries are contained in F. S. Regs., Part II. and the Staff Manual respectively. Title pages will be prepared in manuscript.

WAR DIARY
or
INTELLIGENCE SUMMARY.
(Erase heading not required.)

Place	Date	Hour	Summary of Events and Information	Remarks and references to Appendices
SUPPORT BEAUMONT-HAMEL SECTOR	19/7/18		Trench Mortar activity. Front Line Batts raided enemy posts assisted by heavy barrage at 12.15 AM.	[illegible]
	20/7/18		Fairly quiet. Our artillery shelled BEAUMONT-HAMEL	[illegible]
"	21/7/18		Quiet day.	[illegible]
"	22/7/18		AUCHONVILLERS shelled several times during the day	[illegible]
"	23/7/18		Heavy shelling of our Front Line at 5 A.M. T.M activity at night.	[illegible]
"	24/7/18		Activity normal	[illegible]
"	24/7/18 25/7/18	night of.	Battalion relieved by 1st Bn. [illegible] Regt. & proceed to ARQUEVES staying for the night at LEALVILLERS. In Corps & G.H.Q. reserve.	[illegible]
ARQUEVES	25/7/18		Battn. arrived ARQUEVES at 10-15 AM. The remainder of the day was spent in refitting ~~[illegible]~~ etc.	[illegible]
"	26/7/18		~~Battn.~~ Company training.	[illegible]
"	27/7/18		Battn. firing on range.	[illegible]
"	28/7/18		Company Training.	[illegible]
	29/7/18		Bn. transferred from "V" Corps area into "IV" Corps area & proceed to AUTHIE	[illegible]

D. D. & L., London, E.C.
(A8004) Wt. W1771/M2031 750,000 5/17 Sch. 52 Forms/C2118/14

Instructions regarding War Diaries and Intelligence Summaries are contained in F. S. Regs., Part II. and the Staff Manual respectively. Title pages will be prepared in manuscript.

WAR DIARY

or

INTELLIGENCE SUMMARY.

(Erase heading not required.)

Army Form C. 2118.

Place	Date	Hour	Summary of Events and Information	Remarks and references to Appendices
AUTHIE	30/7/18		Company Training. MAJOR. N.S. CLUTTERBUCK D.S.O. R.M.L.I. taken on the strength of this Bn.	[illegible signature]
"	31/7/18		Company Training.	[illegible signature]

D. D. & L., London, E.C.
(A8004) Wt. W1771/M2031 750,000 5/17 Sch. 52 Forms/C2118/14

WR 27

CONFIDENTIAL.

1st BATTALION ROYAL MARINES.

WAR DIARY.

1st AGUST 1918.

to

31st. Agust. 1918.

PSandilands

Major R.M.L.I.

Commanding 1st Battn. ROYAL MARINES.

To. Headquarters,

188th Inf. Bde

T.10

Instructions regarding War Diaries and Intelligence Summaries are contained in F. S. Regs., Part II. and the Staff Manual respectively. Title pages will be prepared in manuscript.

WAR DIARY
or
~~INTELLIGENCE SUMMARY.~~
(Erase heading not required.)

Army Form C. 2118.

Place	Date	Hour	Summary of Events and Information	Remarks and references to Appendices
AUTHIE	1/8/18.		Bn carried defence scheme of Purple Line in front of COIGNEUX	[illegible]
"	2/8/18.		Bn proceed to Baths & afterwards carried out Company Training.	[illegible]
"	3/8/18.		Instructions in Bivouacs Heavy rain fell	[illegible]
"	4/8/18.		Bn Church parade in morning. 10.15 P.M. Bn moved to VAUCHELLES arriving 12 Midnight	[illegible]
VAUCHELLES	5/8/18		Bn left VAUCHELLES at 5.30 P.M. & marched via LOUVENCOURT to BROWN LINE ~~[illegible]~~ ACHEUX & arrived at 8.30 P.M.	[illegible]
BROWN LINE ACHEUX	6/8/18		Right half Bn worked on defences. Left half Bn carried out attack practise.	[illegible]
"	7/8/18		Left half Bn worked on defences Right half Bn carried out attack practise	[illegible]
	8/8/18		Right half Bn worked on defences. Left half carried out attack practise	[illegible]
			Bn left BROWN LINE at 6.0 pm. & marched via LOUVENCOURT & VARENNES to CONTAY, arriving at 3.0 AM.	[illegible]
	9/8/18.		Bn resting.	[illegible]
	10/8/18		Bn carried out Musketry practise	[illegible]

Contd

A5834 Wt. W4973 M687 750,000 8/16 D. D. & L. Ltd. Forms/C.2118/13.

Instructions regarding War Diaries and Intelligence Summaries are contained in F. S. Regs., Part II. and the Staff Manual respectively. Title pages will be prepared in manuscript.

WAR DIARY

or

INTELLIGENCE SUMMARY.

(Erase heading not required.)

Army Form C. 2118.

Place	Date	Hour	Summary of Events and Information	Remarks and references to Appendices
CONTAY	11/8/18		Bn. Bathed & afterwards attended Church Parade.	[illegible]
"	12/8/18		Bn. in co-operation with remainder of Division carried of attack practise	[illegible]
"	13/8/18		Bn. carried musketery & company training	[illegible]
"	14/8/18		Bn. carried out attack practise. Bn. left CONTAY at 9.20 pm. & arrived HENU at 3.40 A.M. 15/8/18.	[illegible]
HENU	15/8/18		Bn. inspected by O.C. & spent remainder of day digging in huts.	[illegible]
"	16/8/18		Bn. Drill under O.C.	[illegible]
"	17/8/18		Companys carried out attack practise	[illegible]
"	18/8/18		Bn. attended Church Parade & afterwards musketery training.	[illegible]
"	19/8/18		Companys carried out Attack Practise, & at 11.0 pm. left HENU for SOUASTRE.	[illegible]

Con[illegible]

D. D. & L., London, E.C.
(A10266) Wt W5300/P713 750,000 2/18 Sch. 52 Forms/C2118/16

Instructions regarding War Diaries and Intelligence Summaries are contained in F. S. Regs., Part II. and the Staff Manual respectively. Title pages will be prepared in manuscript.

WAR DIARY
or
INTELLIGENCE SUMMARY.

(Erase heading not required.)

Army Form C. 2118.

Place	Date	Hour	Summary of Events and Information	Remarks and references to Appendices
SOUASTRE	20/8/18		Companies inspected & replenished prior to going into action.	
	21/8/18		Battalion marched from Billets in CHATEAU-DE-LA-HAIE Camp to assembly position in old French some 1500 yards west of ABLAIZONVILLE	
British Front Line before ABLAIZONVILLE		4.55 am	At zero 4.55 am Battalion passed through objective of 37th Division and in co-operation with Tanks attacked enemy position	
			OBJECTIVE. Eastern side of LOGEAST WOOD.	
		7.45 am	'C' and 'D' Coys encountered obstinate resistance from enemy Machine Guns at F.3D and 'C' at main road running from ABLAIZONVILLE to ACHIET-LE-GRAND. In order to deal with the situation 'C' Company and 2 Platoons of 'D' Coy were brought down and energetically attacked these positions which were in a very short time cleared of the enemy. 'C' Company and the 2 Platoons of 'D' Coy formed up and carried on with the advance meeting the two remaining Platoons of 'D' Coy and immediately entered the WESTERN edge of LOGEAST WOOD.	
			As a result of this operation one 5.9 Gun, 250 Prisoners and 6 Trench Mortars together with much material were captured	
			During the day from 9 am onwards three strong counter-attacks were made against our positions but were repulsed and in each case with sanguinary loss	
LOGEAST WOOD	22		Our positions were heavily shelled	
			Enemy counter-attacked at 5.10 am but without success.	
		11 am	Enemy again formed up for counter-attack but before he could emerge from his positions the promptitude of our Lewis Gun and Rifle fire broke up the attack.	
	23	[illegible] am	Battalion was relieved by a Battalion of the [illegible] Brigade [illegible] Division and proceeded into BLUE LINE in F.29c.	

D. D. & L., London, E.C.
(A10266) Wt W5300/P713 750,000 2/18 Sch. 52 Forms/C2118/16

Instructions regarding War Diaries and Intelligence Summaries are contained in F. S. Regs., Part II. and the Staff Manual respectively. Title pages will be prepared in manuscript.

WAR DIARY
or
~~INTELLIGENCE SUMMARY.~~

(Erase heading not required.)

Army Form C. 2118.

Place	Date	Hour	Summary of Events and Information	Remarks and references to Appendices
BLUELINE	24.	5.30am	Battalion marched to WESTERN edge of LOUPART WOOD and Bivouacked for the night.	[illegible]
LOUPART WOOD	25.	5.30am	Battalion attacked enemy positions FIRST OBJECTIVE Track running NE from G35.d.5.05 to G36.c20.40. FINAL " Eastern edge of the village of LE BARQUE First objective reached at 5.40 a.m. Final objective reached at 6.30 a.m. and position immediately consolidated Through this operation, 150 prisoners, 2 Trench Mortars and 20 Machine Guns along with much War Material was captured Immediately after gaining our objective, enemy made futile attempts to drive us from our positions but was repulsed with heavy losses. Throughout the day the enemy attempted to mass for counter-attack but the prompt action on the part of our Lewis Gun and Rifle Fire frustrated all attempts and at the end of the day our line was intact.	[illegible]
	26.		Our Patrols were active	[illegible]
	27.		Isolated enemy activity	[illegible]
	28	4.30	Battalion was relieved by 8th Battn MANCHESTERS and proceeded to MIRAUMONT in Bivouacs	[illegible]

Casualties

Killed		Died of Wounds		Wounded		Missing	
Off.	O.Rs.	Off.	O.Rs.	Off.	O.Rs.	Off.	O.Rs.
3.	46		7.	12.	260	–	31

D. D. & L., London, E.C.
(A10266) Wt W5300/P713 750,000 2/15 Sch. 52 Forms/C2118/16

Instructions regarding War Diaries and Intelligence Summaries are contained in F. S. Regs., Part II. and the Staff Manual respectively. Title pages will be prepared in manuscript.

WAR DIARY
or
INTELLIGENCE SUMMARY.
(Erase heading not required.)

Army Form C. 2118.

Place	Date	Hour	Summary of Events and Information	Remarks and references to Appendices
MIRAUMONT	29		Cleaning up & reorganising &c.	
	30		Reorganising, re-equipping &c. Battalion inspected by G.O.C. 188th Inf Bde and at 11.30 p.m. Battalion proceeded to BOIRY-ST-RICTRUDE	[illegible] Lieut
BOIRY ST RICTRUDE	31		Battalion rested.	
			31/8/18 Major RMLI Cmdg 1st Bn Royal Marines	

D. D. & L., London, E.C. (A10266) Wt W5300/P713 750,000 2/18 Sch. 52 Forms/C2118/16

Vol. 28

S E C R E T.

1st B A T T A L I O N   R O Y A L   M A R I N E S.

W A R   D I A R Y.

VOLUME ~~IX.~~ V.

1.9.18.
to
30.9.18.

Sandilands

Lieut.Colonel R.M.L.I.
Commanding 1st Battn. ROYAL MARINES.

To :-.

Instructions regarding War Diaries and Intelligence Summaries are contained in F. S. Regs., Part II. and the Staff Manual respectively. Title pages will be prepared in manuscript.

WAR DIARY
or
~~INTELLIGENCE SUMMARY.~~

(Erase heading not required.)

Army Form C. 2118.

Place	Date	Hour	Summary of Events and Information	Remarks and references to Appendices
BOIRY St RICTRUDE	1/9/18.		Battalion bivouaced in the open arriving at 5.30 A.M. During the day Bn received instructions to move up to an assemble position near FONTAINE in U 7 a ~~[illegible]~~. Battalion left at about 5.45 P.M. arriving about 9. P.M. resting for the night in trench to N.W. of CROISILLES – FONTAINE Rd. Verbal instructions received for the attack on following day.	R.H.P.W.
In Action from U 10 a to QUEANT.	2/9/18.		Battalion moved to assembly position in U 10 a with the 2nd Bn. R.IRISH Regt on left and ANSON in SUPPORT. At ZERO (5 AM) plus 2 hrs. 45 mins Advance was made in artillery formation through RIENCOURT passing through 57th DIV. and attacking 2nd objective – a line running from V25 c 0.1 to V19 d 3.7. Fighting continued throughout the day until final objective was taken and the Bn held a line before QUEANT running from Y26 d 7.9 to Y27 d 5.0. Casualties. Killed 1 officer 15 O.Rs. Wounded 1 officer 61 O.Rs. (estimated).	R.H.P.W.
ditto	3/9/18.		At About 9.30 A.M. Bn. received instructions to proceed to an assemble position in V 28 a & b with orders to stand by to move at short notice. At 7.0. P.M instructions received to proceed to BUISSY SWITCH and HINDENBURG SUPPORT line from junction of Switch & Support line to D 6 c 8 7. and Bn was placed at the disposal of G.O.C 189th Inf. Bde. Killed 13. O.Rs. wounded 14 O.R.	R.H.P.W.
BUISSY SWITCH	4/9/18.		At 1. AM one coy. 'D' Coy was ordered to assist in an attack on the BRIDGEHEAD in E 8 b & d. & at 5 AM another coy 'C' Coy was ordered to assist the HOOD Bn. in an attack on another Bridge Head in E 2 central. Little headway could be made & our troops were forced to withdraw to their original line having suffered heavy casualties. Killed 7. wounded 6. Bn relieved by 190th Bde & whole Bn withdrawn to original line.	R.H.P.W.
ditto	5/9/18.		Bn remained in trenches & was subject to periodical heavy shelling & gas shelling. Casualties Killed 1 officer 1. O.R. Wounded 1 officer & 21. O.R. Divisional Commander visited troops in the line & congratulated all ranks on their most successful operation.	R.H.P.W.

D. D. & L., London, E.C.
(A8004) Wt. W1771/M2031 750,000 5/17 Sch. 52 Forms/C2118/14

Instructions regarding War Diaries and Intelligence Summaries are contained in F. S. Regs., Part II. and the Staff Manual respectively. Title pages will be prepared in manuscript.

WAR DIARY
or
~~INTELLIGENCE SUMMARY.~~
(*Erase heading not required.*)

Army Form C. 2118.

Place	Date	Hour	Summary of Events and Information	Remarks and references to Appendices
BUISSY SWITCH	6/9/18		Bn remained in trenches. Periodical shelling. Wounded 4.	AH
do.	7/9/18		Bn remained in trenches during day. Occasional shelling. Wounded 4. Bn moved at 9.0pm via BULLECOURT to U19d 8.5 (Map 57C SW) arriving about midnight. The night was spent here.	AH
U19d 8.5	8/9/18		At 7-30 pm Bn left halting place and marched to BOYELLES entraining there about 11.0pm. Night of 8/9th spent in train	AH
GOUY-EN-ARTOIS	9/9/18		Bn arrived by train at LAHERLIERE at 7.0am & marched to billets in GOUY-EN-ARTOIS arriving there at 8-30am. Forenoon occupied by Bn resting, afternoon by cleaning up.	AH
do	10/9/18		Cleaning, re equipping and inspections.	AH
do	11/9/18		Platoon training.	AH
do	12/9/18		Company training and musketry on range	AH
do	13/9/18		Training	AH
do	14/9/18		Inspection of Battn by Brig. Gen. J.D. Coleridge in morning. Brigadier inspected transport.	AH
do	15th (Sunday)		Church Parade in morning. Lecture to officers & NCOs on "Submarine Warfare" by Lt. Comdr RN.	AH
do	16		Training.	AH
do	17		Bn left GOUY at 10-30 am and proceeded by march route to BLAIREVILLE where night was spent.	AH
	18		Bn left BLAIREVILLE by march route at 9.0am for bivouacs in T30 b & T24 d (57C SW). Brigade scheme en route, attacking CROISILLES and ST LEGER from BOYELLES. RM Bn on right, 2nd ROYAL IRISH REGT centre and ANSON Bn on left. Bn arrived at bivouacs at 3.0pm. Bivouacs taken over from 6th Bn KINGS LIVERPOOLS.	AH

D. D. & L., London, E.C.
(A8001) Wt. W1771/M2031 750,000 5/17 Sch. 52 Forms/C2118/14

Army Form C. 2118.

Instructions regarding War Diaries and Intelligence Summaries are contained in F. S. Regs., Part II. and the Staff Manual respectively. Title pages will be prepared in manuscript.

WAR DIARY
or
~~INTELLIGENCE SUMMARY.~~

(Erase heading not required.)

Place	Date	Hour	Summary of Events and Information	Remarks and references to Appendices
N^r CROISILLES	19/9/18		B^n in bivouacs at T30 b & T24 d (South of CROISILLES) Platoon & company training and range practice	HH HH
do	20/9/18		Training Companies in attack & Lewis Guns on range	HH
do	21/9/18		do	HH
do	22/9/18		do	HH
do	23		do Batt^n in practice attack on HENDECOURT	HH
do	24		do	HH
do	25		do	

D. D. & L., London, E.C.
(A8001) Wt. W1771/M2031 750,000 5/17 Sch. 52 Forms/C2118/14

Instructions regarding War Diaries and Intelligence Summaries are contained in F. S. Regs., Part II. and the Staff Manual respectively. Title pages will be prepared in manuscript.

WAR DIARY
or
INTELLIGENCE SUMMARY.
(Erase heading not required.)

Army Form C. 2118.

Place	Date	Hour	Summary of Events and Information	Remarks and references to Appendices
CROISILLES.	26/9/18.		63rd R.N. Division in bivouacs SOUTH of CROISILLES. – 1st Bn ROYAL MARINES move off companies 200 yds. distance at 1.45 pm. along road to QUEANT arriving at 4.45 am. where Battalion move into trenches S.W. of QUEANT in D-7-b-6. At 12.15 am. the Bn. moved to assembly position N.W. of MOEUVRES.	HH
In action over the CANAL du NORD	27/9/18		Zero hour at 5.20 am. The 52nd Division advance to high ground EAST of CANAL du NORD 190th Brigade advance and mop up "THE HINDENBURG LINE." followed by the 188th Bde. 189th Bde in support. – The 1st Bn. ROYAL MARINES move at zero + 20 minutes. ANSON Bn on left with ROYAL IRISH REGT in support – Reaching E 16 d and E 21 B the Bn. swing S. EAST and move to the attack on the village of ANNEUX. Strong opposition was met with at the FACTORY between ANNEUX and GRAINCOURT but was overcome with heavy loss to the enemy in personnel and material. The village of ANNEUX was captured at 2.30 pm. and the line consolidated. At 6.45 pm the enemy counter attacked under a heavy machine gun barrage but was repulsed with heavy loss. The enemy left many killed – the remainder of the night passed off quietly. Casualties killed – Officers 4 other ranks [illegible] Wounded Officers 6 other ranks 91 Captures 2 heavy howitzers 9 field guns	HH
ANNEUX.	28/9/18		The 57th Division pass through the 63rd R.N. Division at 6.30 am and advance on FONTAINE-NOTRE-DAME and CANTAING on to the CANAL de l'ESCAUT. – The 1st Bn. ROYAL MARINES reorganize behind ANNEUX and at 3 pm move into trench between FONTAINE and CANTAING in F. 22 central. At nightfall the 189th Bde. move up to cross the CANAL de l'ESCAUT and the River ESCAUT.	HH

(A8001) Wt. W1771/M2031 750,000 5/17 Sch. 52 Forms/C2118/14 D. D. & L., London, E.C.

Army Form C. 2118.

WAR DIARY
or
~~INTELLIGENCE SUMMARY.~~
(Erase heading not required.)

Instructions regarding War Diaries and Intelligence Summaries are contained in F. S. Regs., Part II. and the Staff Manual respectively. Title pages will be prepared in manuscript.

Place	Date	Hour	Summary of Events and Information	Remarks and references to Appendices
Between FONTAINE and CANTAING	29/9/18		The 1st Bn ROYAL MARINES move at 11.30 am and cross the RIVER ESCAUT and THE CANAL de L'ESCAUT, and line up for an attack on high ground A26 b.d. Assembly position in F30-A (sheet 57c NE) The Bn attacked at 1.45 pm but met with heavy opposition from the direction of PROVILLE. Heavy enfilade fire rendered progress very slow. At nightfall line ran A26 a and A19 d (sheet 57b NW) Casualties :- Officers wounded 3 ORs KILLED 16 WOUNDED 112.	HH
High ground overlooking PROVILLE and Fy de PARIS	30/9/18		The 57th Division advance to the attack and leapfrog through the 63 RN Division. Heavy opposition was met with, and at places our front line was barely reached. Casualties :- ORs killed 2 wounded 30.	HH
do	1/10/18		At 10.30 pm 'D' Coy in conjunction with a coy of the ANSON Bn move off to capture and consolidate the strong point in A27 a. The strong point was reached and positions consolidated. At 6.10 am the enemy counter attacked heavily with the result that 'D' Coy was forced to withdraw to trench in A27 a 2 1 where owing to heavy machine gun fire this party was isolated and no assistance could be sent. At 5.44 pm the 52nd Division advance under a heavy barrage where pushing on as far as possible they would automatically relieve the 63rd RN Division. The Bn ROYAL SCOTS FUSILIERS passed through the 1st Bn "ROYAL MARINES" and reached and consolidated on a line approx. A20 d and A27 a Casualties up to time of relief 1 Officer wounded - ORs Wounded 8 At 8.30 pm the 1st Bn ROYAL MARINES form up on road A20c - A19.d and move to bivouacs in F26 a 3.1 (Sheet 57c NE. Total missing during operations 59. ORs	HH

D. D. & L., London, E.C. (A8001) Wt. W1771/M2031 750,000 5/17 Sch. 52 Forms/C2118/14

CONFIDENTIAL –

Nol 29

1st Battalion ROYAL MARINES. –

War Diary –

VOL. VI

OCTOBER 1st to 31st, 1918. –

To Headquarters
188th Inf. Bde

A 739

Standilands
Lt. Col. RMLI.
Cmdg 1st Bn Royal Marines.

Army Form C. 2118.

Instructions regarding War Diaries and Intelligence Summaries are contained in F. S. Regs., Part II. and the Staff Manual respectively. Title pages will be prepared in manuscript.

WAR DIARY
or
INTELLIGENCE SUMMARY.
(Erase heading not required.)

Place	Date	Hour	Summary of Events and Information	Remarks and references to Appendices
High ground overlooking PROVILLE and FBG. de PARIS	1918 Oct 1st		At 10-30 pm Sept 30th D Coy in conjunction with a coy of the ANSON BATTN moved off to capture and consolidate the strong point in A27a (Sheet 57c NW). The strong point was reached and position consolidated. At 6.10am Oct 1st the enemy counter attacked heavily with the result that D Coy were forced to withdraw to the [illegible] in A27a 2.1 [illegible] owing to heavy machine gun fire this party was isolated and no assistance could be sent. At 3.40 pm the 52nd (Lowland) Division advanced under a heavy barrage to [illegible] as far as possible. They would automatically relieve the 63rd (RN) Division. The 4th ROYAL SCOTS FUSILIERS passed through the 1st Bn ROYAL MARINES and [illegible] and consolidated a line running approximately A20d and A27d. Casualties up to time of relief Off wounded 1 ORs wounded 8. At 8-20 pm the 1st Bn ROYAL MARINES formed up on road A20c A19d and moved to bivouacs in F2b a 2.1 (Sheet 57c NE) near ANNEUX	HH
Nr ANNEUX	2nd		Day spent in digging in of bivouacs & tents, cleaning up & reorganising	HH
do	3rd		Inspections & reorganising	HH
do	4th		Company training in forenoon	HH
do	5th		do	HH
do	6th (Sunday)		Church parade. At about 6.30 pm enemy shell fell in camp and killed 1 and wounded 3 ORs. About 9.0 pm enemy aircraft bombed camp & wounded 11 ORs and killed 5 horses.	HH
do	7th		At 4.0 pm Bn moved off from bivouacs to assembly position in G8c via Nos [illegible] Bridge over L'ESCAUT river and by No 12 bridge over the CANAL de ST QUENTIN. Battalion was in position by 19-30. Companies fell in after a hot meal	HH
	8th		on the RUMILLY ROAD crossing the starting point G8.d.3.0 at 01.10 hours and moved to jumping off position in G6 a & c	HH

(A7092). Wt W12839/M1293 75,000. 1/17. D. D. & L., Ltd. Forms/C.2118/14.

Instructions regarding War Diaries and Intelligence Summaries are contained in F. S. Regs., Part II. and the Staff Manual respectively. Title pages will be prepared in manuscript.

WAR DIARY
or
INTELLIGENCE SUMMARY.
(Erase heading not required.)

Army Form C. 2118.

Place	Date	Hour	Summary of Events and Information	Remarks and references to Appendices
G16 a & c	1918 Oct 8th Contd.		Companies were lined out immediately in rear of the 2nd Bn ROYAL IRISH REGT. in two waves A on right B on left of first wave C on right D on left of second wave Artillery formation covered Brigade front from G10 c3.0 to G16 d9.7 [illegible] [illegible] was completed by 0450 hrs without casualties. At 0430 hours barrage opened. At 0450 barrage lifted & 2nd Bn ROYAL IRISH REGT. moved to attack followed by 1st Bn ROYAL MARINES. The 2nd R.I. REGT captured first objective on schedule time. Immediately in rear of this objective, trench running through G6 c & d, 1st Bn ROYAL MARINES shook out into attack formation, and advanced to attack of 2nd objective road running from A30c to H1c. Attack progressed satisfactorily with few casualties until right edge of village of NIERGNIES and CEMETERY in H.1 were reached. At these points heavy fighting occurred & severe casualties inflicted on the enemy holding the cemetery which was held by numerous MGs. Tanks materially assisted in the clearing of this cemetery. The attack continued to LA BELLE ETOILE which was found to be strongly held by MGs & infantry. The first a frontal attack failed. 'D' Coy immediately attacked on left & B coy on right, succeeded in enveloping the position & captured 4 MGs & about 30 of the enemy. All objectives were gained by 0810 hours & touch obtained with K.R.R.s on right & HOOD Bn on left.	[initials]

D. D. & L., London, E.C. (A8001) Wt. W1771/M2031 750,000 5/17 Sch. 52 Forms/C2118/14

Instructions regarding War Diaries and Intelligence Summaries are contained in F. S. Regs., Part II. and the Staff Manual respectively. Title pages will be prepared in manuscript.

WAR DIARY
or
INTELLIGENCE SUMMARY.
(*Erase heading not required.*)

Army Form C. 2118.

Place	Date	Hour	Summary of Events and Information	Remarks and references to Appendices
Nr HIERGNIES	1918 Oct 8th contd.		At 0830 hrs the enemy counter attacked using captured British Tanks & forced the troops on our right flank to withdraw. Efforts were made to form a defensive flank but the enemy forced our forward posts back about 200 yards. Our troops were immediately reorganised & assisted by the barrage recaptured all objectives. At 1300 hrs the enemy opened up an intense bombardment on our troops holding the cemetery for an hour. This was repeated throughout the afternoon, making the position untenable. At 16 30 the enemy counter attacked heavily & heavy fighting ensued. At this time a Bn of the EAST SURREY REGT were about to relieve but this was delayed until the situation was cleared up. By 17 30 hours our troops had been forced back to a line H.1.C.4.5. along road through H1.C. to G.6.a.5.0 along track to A.30.d.8.5. This was reported & instructions received for the EAST SURREYS to push forward & take over the line & our troops to withdraw when this had been done. This was done & the Bn withdrawn at 0001 hrs & marched back to bivouacs near ANNEUX. Total Casualties Killed 2 Offs. 9 ORs. Wounded 4 Offs 82 ORs unaccounted for 48 ORs. Captures 2 Field guns 12 MGs. Prisoners captured approx. 100	N.H.

D. D. & L., London, E.C. (A8001) Wt. W1771/M2031 750,000 5/17 Sch. 52 Forms/C2118/14

Army Form C. 2118.

WAR DIARY
or
INTELLIGENCE SUMMARY.

(Erase heading not required.)

Instructions regarding War Diaries and Intelligence Summaries are contained in F. S. Regs., Part II. and the Staff Manual respectively. Title pages will be prepared in manuscript.

Place	Date	Hour	Summary of Events and Information	Remarks and references to Appendices
	Oct 9th		Bn left bivouacs near ANNEUX at 11-30 & proceeded by march route to MORCHIES arriving at 16 30	HH
MORCHIES	10th		Bn in bivouacs.	HH
	11th		Bn left MORCHIES & entrained at VAULX VRAUCOURT at 15 30 hrs.	HH
PIERREMONT	12th		Bn detrained at ST POL midnight & marched to Billets at PIERREMONT and LIBESSART arriving 0200 hrs.	HH
do	13-21		Training	HH
	22nd		Bn left PIERREMONT 0900 hrs & proceeded by march route via ST POL to AMBRINES arriving at 14 30 hrs.	HH
AMBRINES	23-29		Training.	HH
do	30		do Bn Gymkhana in afternoon.	HH
do	31		do Transport left for new area.	HH

D. D. & L., London, E.C.
(A8001) Wt. W1771/M2031 750,000 5/17 Sch. 52 Forms/C2118/14

C O N F I D E N T I A L.

VR 30

1st Battalion ROYAL MARINES.

- W A R D I A R Y. -

Vol. V11.

NOVEMBER 1st -- 30th 1918.

N B Cartwright

Commanding

Lieut. Colonel R.M.L.I.
1st Battalion Royal Marines.

a/26

Headquarters,
188th Infantry Brigade.

Instructions regarding War Diaries and Intelligence Summaries are contained in F. S. Regs., Part II. and the Staff Manual respectively. Title pages will be prepared in manuscript.

WAR DIARY
or
INTELLIGENCE SUMMARY.

(*Erase heading not required.*)

Army Form C. 2118.

Place	Date	Hour	Summary of Events and Information	Remarks and references to Appendices
AMBRINES	1918 Nov 1st		1st Bn ROYAL MARINES marched from AMBRINES at 0830 hrs to MAZIERES where it embussed at 0930 hours and proceeded via LENS to EVIN-MALMAISON (about 5 miles N of DOUAI arriving there at 1500 hrs. Battalion in billets.	H.H.
EVIN-MALMAISON	2-4		Training	H.H.
Morning	5th		Bn left EVIN at 0730 hours and proceeded by bus to billets in HAULCHIN (5 miles S.W. of VALENCIENNES)	H.H.
do	6th		Battn marched from HAULCHIN to AULNOY. In billets	H.H.
do	7th		Bn marched from AULNOY to SAULTAIN, halted there for four hours and proceeded to SEBOURQUIAUX. In billets	H.H.
do	8th		Bn left SEBOURQUIAUX and marched to ANGRE, halting there about 2 hours and continued to billets in AUDREGNIES.	H.H.
do.	9th		Bn marched from AUDREGNIES to BLAUGIES. Halted there for four hours and marched to SARS LA BRUYERE. In billets	H.H.
Active Operations	10th		The Bn Moved from SARS LA BRUYERE at 0600 hrs on morning of 10th inst with instructions to proceed to BOUGNIES & a warning note was received that the Bn would probably pass through 190th Inf. Bde at 12 noon and proceed to the attack. During the march a conference was assembled consisting of all Bn Commanders & verbal instructions were given for the attack. The Bn arrived at BOUGNIES at 1000 hrs on the return of the	R.H.P.W.

D. D. & L., London, E.C.
(A8004) Wt. W1771/M2031 750,000 5/17 Sch. 52 Forms/C2118/14

Instructions regarding War Diaries and Intelligence Summaries are contained in F. S. Regs., Part II. and the Staff Manual respectively. Title pages will be prepared in manuscript.

WAR DIARY
or
INTELLIGENCE SUMMARY.
(Erase heading not required.)

Army Form C. 2118.

Place	Date	Hour	Summary of Events and Information	Remarks and references to Appendices
10/11/18 Action Operations	10/11/18		Commanding Officer's Conference of all Officers of the Battalion was held. On verbal instructions issued by the Brigade Commander the ~~[illegible] Bde. ANSON Bn~~ Bde. was ordered to attack and establish a line EAST of VILLERS St GHISLAIN + St SYMPHORIEN. ANSON Bn on the RIGHT, 2nd Bn R.I. Regt on the LEFT, 1st Bn Royal MARINES in SUPPORT. The ~~Bde Group~~ Bde Group accordingly moved to ASQUILLIES arriving at about 11.15 hrs. 2nd R.I. Regt moved up ASQUILLIES–NOUVELLES Rd. ANSON Bn to a SUNKEN Rd in W 7 a + b. Before the Bn cleared the village of ASQUILLIES the enemy opened up a concentrated bombardment on the village inflicting a few casualties. The Bn then moved into the Sunken Rd vacated by the ANSON Bn. Opposition was expected on the LEFT flank + consequently in accordance with previous instructions the Bn moved to NOUVELLES in artillery formation suffering four casualties – Lt Col P SANDILANDS DSO + 3 O.R's.	R.H.P.W.
Wounded			Capt R.A.P. WEST M.C. then took command of the Bn until the arrival of Major F.B.A. LAWRIE from the transport lines. The advance of the Brigade was held up close EAST of NOUVELLES and 1 Company 1st R.M. Bn was placed at the disposal of O.C. 2nd Bn R.I. Regt but was not used. Under cover of Darkness ANSON Bn + 2nd R.I. Regt were able to continue the	

D. D. & L., London, E.C.
(A8004) Wt. W1771/M2031 750,000 5/17 Sch. 52 Forms/C2118/14

Army Form C. 2118.

Instructions regarding War Diaries and Intelligence Summaries are contained in F. S. Regs., Part II. and the Staff Manual respectively. Title pages will be prepared in manuscript.

WAR DIARY
or
INTELLIGENCE SUMMARY.
(Erase heading not required.)

Place	Date	Hour	Summary of Events and Information	Remarks and references to Appendices
[illegible]	10/11/18		Advance establishing a line EAST of SPIENNES + HARMIGNIES by 0530 hrs	RHM
			At about 2330 hrs the Bn received instructions to attack & establish a line EAST of	
ditto	11/11/18		VILLAGES of HARMIGNIES VILLERS ST GHISLAIN. At 0700 hrs further instructions	
			were received that hostilities would cease at 1100 hrs but the objectives established	
			the Bn [illegible] ordered if possible but [illegible] the effect	
			of operation was met the advance was not to be continued. In accordance with	
			these instructions the Bn moved to the attack C Coy on the RIGHT A Coy on the LEFT	
			followed by D in support of C Coy & B Coy in support of D Coy. The [illegible] was commenced	RHM
			at 0500 hrs & was rapid no [illegible] met with. By 10.45 hrs the Bn	
			had passed through the ANSON + 2nd RTP and consolidated its objective. On	
			hostilities ceasing an outpost line was established by B + C Coys [illegible]	
			[illegible] + touch was obtained with	
			the 157th Bde on the RIGHT & the CANADIANS on the LEFT. A + D Coys were	
			billeted in the village of VILLERS ST GHISLAIN + held in support	
			[illegible] the time of the armistice & no further incidents took place	

D. D. & L., London, E.C.
(A8001) Wt. W1771/M2031 750,000 5/17 Sch. 52 Forms/C2118/14

Army Form C. 2118.

Instructions regarding War Diaries and Intelligence Summaries are contained in F. S. Regs., Part II. and the Staff Manual respectively. Title pages will be prepared in manuscript.

WAR DIARY
or
INTELLIGENCE SUMMARY.
(Erase heading not required.)

Place	Date	Hour	Summary of Events and Information	Remarks and references to Appendices
[VIL]LERS ST [G]HISLAIN	12/11/18		A & D Coys relieved B & C in the outpost line	H.H.
	13		B & C " " A & D " " "	H.H.
"	14		A & D " " B & C " " "	H.H.
"	15		ANSON BATTN relieved 1st RM BATTN in outpost line.	H.H.
"	16		Cleaning up and training.	H.H.
"	17		do	H.H.
"	18		do	H.H.
move	19		1st RM BATTN moved from VILLERS ST GHISLAIN to ST SYMPHORIEN.	H.H.
do	20		Bn moved back to VILLERS ST GHISLAIN.	H.H.
[VIL]LERS ST GHISLAIN	21		Training	H.H.
"	22		do	H.H.
"	23		do	H.H.
"	24		Church Parade.	H.H.
"	25-6		Training	H.H.
EUGIES	27		Bn left VILLERS ST GHISLAIN 8.45 and marched via HARMIGNIES – HARVENG, NOIRCHAIN GENLY to EUGIES arriving at 1300 hrs. In billets	H.H.
	28-30		Training (ceremonial etc)	H.H.

D. D. & L., London, E.C.
(A8004) Wt. W1771/M2031 750,000 5/17 Sch. 52 Forms/C2118/14

C O N F I D E N T I A L

WR 31

1st BATTALION ROYAL MARINES.

W A R D I A R Y

Vol.8.

December 1st to 31st 1918.

N. S. L. [illegible]

Lieut. Colonel., R.M.L.I.,
Commanding 1st Battalion Royal Marines.

Adjutant General.
Brigade.
Base Records.
Retain.

Instructions regarding War Diaries and Intelligence Summaries are contained in F. S. Regs., Part II. and the Staff Manual respectively. Title pages will be prepared in manuscript.

WAR DIARY
or
INTELLIGENCE SUMMARY.
(Erase heading not required.)

Army Form C. 2118.

Place	Date	Hour	Summary of Events and Information	Remarks and references to Appendices
	~~1/12/18~~		~~Church Parade~~	
EUGIES	2/12/18		Ceremonial Drill in the morning — Sports in the afternoon.	[illegible]
	3/12/18		Training — Honours & awards — M.C. to Lt A.G. Bareham. M.M. to P.17970 L/C Iw Childs	[illegible]
	"		M.M. to Pte 16495 L/C W Courtnand. & Po 2090 Pte F Lock.	[illegible]
	4/12/18		Training & Sports	[illegible]
	5 - 6th		— " — — " —	[illegible]
	7 8th		— " — Inspection by Div Commdr.	[illegible]
	8 9th		Church parade	[illegible]
	9th		Training — Court of Enquiry re Bombing accident	[illegible]
	10th		— " — & Education	[illegible]
	11th		— " — — " —	[illegible]
LA BOUVERIE	12th		Part of Bn moved to La Bouverie:	[illegible]
	13th 14th		Training	[illegible]
	15th		Church Parade	[illegible]
	16th - 18th		Training & Education	[illegible]
	19th		" Route march	[illegible]
	20th		" & Salvage work	[illegible]
	21st		" — " —	[illegible]
	22nd		Church parade	[illegible]
	23 & 24th		Training	[illegible]
	25th		Church Parade.	[illegible]
	26th		Roll call & Dismiss	[illegible]
	27th		Training	[illegible]
	28th		— " —	[illegible]
	29th		Church Parade.	[illegible]
	30th		Training	[illegible]
	31st		— " —	[illegible]

D. D. & L., London, E.C.
(A8001) Wt. W1771/M2031 750,000 5/17 Sch. 52 Forms/C2118/14

VR 32

C O N F I D E N T I A L.

1st BN. ROYAL MARINES.

War Diary

Vol.9.

January 31st 1919.

Adjutant General.
Brigade.
Base Records.
Retain.

Lieut Colonel. R.M.L.I.,
Commanding 1st Battn Royal Marines.

Instructions regarding War Diaries and Intelligence Summaries are contained in F. S. Regs., Part II. and the Staff Manual respectively. Title pages will be prepared in manuscript.

WAR DIARY
or
INTELLIGENCE SUMMARY.
(Erase heading not required.)

1st Battn. ROYAL MARINES

Army Form C. 2118.

Place	Date	Hour	Summary of Events and Information	Remarks and references to Appendices
LA BOUVERIE AND EUGIES. BELGIUM.	1919 JAN 1st		Training.	H.H.
	2nd		Battalion drill and Education.	H.H.
	3rd		Route march and Education. Court of Inquiry re illegal absence of Ch.858 Pte F. Biddlestone Po.1956 Pte J. Leka and Ch. 742 Pte J. McKnight.	H.H.
	4th		Company training.	H.H.
	5th		Church Parade. Band Concert in afternoon.	H.H.
	6th		Battalion Drill and Education.	H.H.
	7th		Bathing.	H.H.
	7th		Company training and Education.	H.H.
	8th		Training and Education.	H.H.
	9th		Route March.	H.H.
	10th		Company training & Education.	H.H.
	11th		Church Parade. Band Concert in afternoon.	H.H.
	12th		Lecture to Battalion by M.O.	H.H.
	13th		Baths. Honours D.C.M. awarded to Po.675(S) W.O. II F.F.C WINDYBANK.	H.H.
	14th		Company training and education.	H.H.
	15th		Battalion Drill and education.	H.H.
	16th		Route March.	H.H.
	17th		Company training and education.	H.H.
	18th		Church parade.	H.H.
	19th		Company training and education.	H.H.
	20th		Baths.	H.H.
	21st		Company training and education.	H.H.
	22nd		Inspection by C.O. of Battalion by companies.	H.H.
	23rd		Route March and education.	H.H.
	24th			H.H.

D. D. & L., London, E.C.
(A8004) Wt. W1771/M2031 750,000 5/17 Sch. 52 Forms/C2118/14

Instructions regarding War Diaries and Intelligence Summaries are contained in F. S. Regs., Part II. and the Staff Manual respectively. Title pages will be prepared in manuscript.

WAR DIARY
or
~~INTELLIGENCE SUMMARY.~~
(Erase heading not required.)

Army Form C. 2118.

1st Battn ROYAL MARINES

Place	Date	Hour	Summary of Events and Information	Remarks and references to Appendices
LA BOUVERIE AND EUGIES BELGIUM	1919 JAN. 25th		Lecture by C.O. on "RECONSTRUCTION" Ply/1515(S) Sgt. B.G. VICARS and Ply/1559 CPL. J.W. PADLEY awarded M.S.M.	H.H.
	26th		Church Parade	H.H.
	27		Company training and education	H.H.
	28		Baths	H.H.
	29		Company training & Education	H.H.
	30th		Companies reorganised into 2 platoons per Coy. Education	H.H.
	31st		Company training and Education.	H.H.

D. D. & L., London, E.C.
(A8001) Wt. W1771/M2031 750,000 5/17 Sch. 52 Forms/C2118/14

Adjutant General,
3rd Echelon,
G.H.Q.

6

Herewith Army Form C 2118 for February 1919, please.

1ST BATTALION ROYAL MARINES.
No. A 211
Date 3/3/19.

H Horne

Lieut + A Adjt

for O.C. 1/Batt Royal Marines

63

WO 33

CONFIDENTIAL.

1st. BN. ROYAL MARINES.

War Diary

Vol. 10.

FEBRUARY, 1919.

Adjutant General.
Brigade.
Base Records.
Retain.

[signature]
Lieut. Colonel, R.M.L.I.,
Commanding 1st. Bn. ROYAL MARINES.

Instructions regarding War Diaries and Intelligence Summaries are contained in F. S. Regs., Part II. and the Staff Manual respectively. Title pages will be prepared in manuscript.

WAR DIARY
or
INTELLIGENCE SUMMARY.
(*Erase heading not required.*)

Army Form C. 2118.

1st Battn ROYAL MARINES

Place	Date	Hour	Summary of Events and Information	Remarks and references to Appendices
	1919 FEB			
EUGIES	1st		Training & education	HH
&	2nd		Church parade	HH
LA BOUVERIE	3rd		Training & education	HH
BELGIUM	4th		Bathing	HH
	5th		Guard drill & education	HH
	6th		Training & education	HH
	7th		Route march & education	HH
	8th		Lecture to Battalion on "Industrial Problems" by Chaplain	HH
	9th		Church Parade	HH
	10th		Training & Education	HH
	11th		Bathing 1st Class Army Certificate of Education Examination at DOUR	HH
	12th		Guards drill & education	HH
	13th		Company training & education	HH
	14th		Route March & Education	HH
	15		Lecture to Battalion on "Future of Education" by Chaplain	HH
	16		Church Parade	HH
	17th		Training & education	HH
	18th		Bathing	HH
	19		Training & education	HH
	20		do	HH
	21		do	HH
	22		do	HH
	23		Church Parade	HH
	24		Training & education	HH
	25		Bathing	HH
	26		Training & education	HH
	27		do 2nd & 3rd Class Army Certificate of Education examination at PATURAGES	HH
	28		do	HH

D. D. & L., London, E.C.
(A8001) Wt. W1771/M2031 750,000 5/17 Sch. 52 Forms/C2118/14

C O N F I D E N T I A L.

Vol 34

1st Bn ROYAL MARINES.

War Diary.

Vol. 11.

March, 1918.

Adjutant General, R.M.
Brigade,
Base Records,
Retain. ✓

N B Lutchell

Lieut. Colonel, R.M.L.I.
Commanding 1st Bn. ROYAL MARINES.

Army Form C. 2118.

WAR DIARY
or
INTELLIGENCE SUMMARY.
(Erase heading not required.)

Instructions regarding War Diaries and Intelligence Summaries are contained in F. S. Regs., Part II. and the Staff Manual respectively. Title pages will be prepared in manuscript.

1st/Bn ROYAL MARINES.

Place	Date	Hour	Summary of Events and Information	Remarks and references to Appendices
	1919 Mar 1st		[illegible] training.	H.H.
LABOUVERIE	2		Church Parade	H.H.
BELGIUM	3		Training & Education.	H.H.
	4		Bathing	H.H.
	5–8th		Training & Education.	H.H.
	9th		Church Parade.	H.H.
	10th		Training & Education.	H.H.
	11th		Bathing	H.H.
	12–15th		Company training.	H.H.
	16th		Church Parade	H.H.
	17th		Training	H.H.
	18		Baths.	H.H.
	19–22		Training	H.H.
	23		Church Parade	H.H.
	24		Training	H.H.
	25		Bathing	H.H.
	26–29		Training	H.H.
	30		Sunday but no church Parade.	H.H.
	31		Training	

D. D. & L., London, E.C. (A8001) Wt. W1771/M2031 750,000 5/17 Sch. 52 Forms/C2118/14

CONFIDENTIAL.

Vol 35

1st. Battn. ROYAL MARINES.

WAR DIARY

Vol. 12.

APRIL, 1919.

Adjutant General, R.M.
Brigade.
Base Records.
Retain.

N.S. Clutterbuck

Lieut.Colonel, R.M.L.I.,
Commanding 1st. Bn. ROYAL MARINES.

Instructions regarding War Diaries and Intelligence Summaries are contained in F. S. Regs., Part II. and the Staff Manual respectively. Title pages will be prepared in manuscript.

Army Form C. 2118.

WAR DIARY
or
INTELLIGENCE SUMMARY.
(Erase heading not required.)

1/Bn. Royal Marines

Place	Date 1919	Hour	Summary of Events and Information	Remarks and references to Appendices
La Bouverie	April 1		Baths	[illegible]
Belgium	2-4		Company Training	[illegible]
	5		Training	[illegible]
	6		Church Parade	[illegible]
	7		Training	[illegible]
	8		Baths	[illegible]
	9-12		Training	[illegible]
	13		Church Parade	[illegible]
	14-15		Company Training	[illegible]
	16		Baths	[illegible]
	17		Training	[illegible]
	18.		Roll Call	[illegible]
	19		Kit Inspection	[illegible]
	20		Church Parade	[illegible]
	21		Roll Call	[illegible]
	22		Training	[illegible]
	23		Baths	[illegible]
	24-26		Company Training	[illegible]
	27		Church Parade	[illegible]
	28-29		Training	[illegible]
	30		Baths	[illegible]

D. D. & L., London, E.C.
(A8004) Wt. W1771/M2031 750,000 5/17 Sch. 52 Forms/C2118/14

www.ingramcontent.com/pod-product-compliance
Lightning Source LLC
Chambersburg PA
CBHW081404160426
43193CB00013B/2101